Early Literary
Magazines
of
Texas

Early Literary Magazines of Texas

BY IMOGENE BENTLEY DICKEY

North Texas State University

STECK-VAUGHN COMPANY   AUSTIN, TEXAS

An Intext *Publisher*

ISBN   0-8114-7717-7
Library of Congress Catalog Card Number 78-120141
Copyright © 1970 by Steck-Vaughn Company, Austin, Texas

To
Susan B. Riley
With Affection and Gratitude

Contents

Author's Acknowledgments

During the many years that I have been interested in and worked on early Texas magazines, I have become indebted to many. I shall always be grateful to Dr. Susan B. Riley, my professor and friend, who first directed me to research in the periodical field. To Sheila Aden Higgins and Dr. James Ward Lee for their interest and encouragement, I acknowledge a special indebtedness. I am also most appreciative of the help received from the many librarians with whom I worked. Not last in my appreciation are the members of my family, whose interest also contributed to this volume.

Introduction

According to Frank Luther Mott, an examination of American magazines and an investigation into their history show that their importance rests upon three services: first, the magazines provide a literature which can be called democratic and is sometimes of high quality; second, they are of economic importance to literature, for contributors are paid more or less adequately, and magazines stimulate the book trade; third, the files of the magazines furnish an invaluable history of our times.[1] A study of early Texas literary magazines shows that these three services, especially the third, were important in Texas.

The term magazine is here defined as a stitched or stapled publication with a cover, issued regularly and containing a variety of subject matter designed to entertain and enlighten. By literary magazine is meant all those periodicals whose editors declare their purpose to be literary, all those spoken of as literary by other editors, and all those published for the home which contain essays, poems, stories—magazines so classified because of content.

Over three hundred periodicals published in Texas from 1858 (the date of the earliest literary magazine that could be found) to 1929 have been located and studied. The many religious periodicals, professional and student publications, bulletins, studies, official organs, and art, advertising, historical, and local commercial publications were excluded. After these exclusions, there remained forty periodicals published in Texas between 1858 and 1929 which met the definition of a literary magazine. It cannot be said that these forty periodicals are all the literary magazines published in Texas from 1858 to 1929. It may be said, however, that these are all that could be found in the major libraries. It may also be said that, although this list is not exhaustive, it is representative.

It is probable that many magazines published in Texas in the

---

1. Frank Luther Mott, *A History of American Magazines 1741-1850* (Cambridge: Harvard University Press, 1939), pp. 2-3.

nineteenth century and the first quarter of the twentieth century never found their way into a library and so may never be found. There were references in the available magazines to other magazines which could not be located. It is only in recent years that The University of Texas at Austin, which has the largest collection of Texas periodicals, has emphasized the importance of the Texas Collection and made a great effort to collect and preserve the early Texas periodicals. The Texas Collection at Baylor University, Waco, Texas, and that at the Houston Public Library are also stressing the importance of the early Texas periodicals and collecting and preserving them.

This tardy recognition of the importance of the value of periodicals as historical records of their time has resulted not only in the loss of some magazines, but also in incomplete files of those preserved. When magazines were located, it was surprising to note how incomplete the files were. Unbroken files were found for only eleven of the magazines. Of ten others only one issue could be found. When it was possible to reconstruct from the files the life story of a magazine, it was nearly always a story of a short life filled with difficulties; but whether complete or only suggested, the story of the magazine was always interesting.

One of the earliest magazines published in Texas, *Texas Journal of Education,* was not a literary magazine. It was, as its name indicates, an educational magazine, first published in Houston in July, 1854, only nine years after Texas was admitted as a state. The magazine had its beginning at the first Texas State Educational Convention, which opened in Huntsville, July 16, 1854. The one copy located, Volume I, Number 1, in the Texas Collection at The University of Texas at Austin, is a record of a part of the educational development of the state; but it is impossible to ascertain how long the journal was published or what finally became of it. Its importance can only be imagined; but the publication of an educational journal at such an early date attests to the truth that education in the early years of statehood was of special interest to the people of Texas. This concern for education could have been in part responsible for the concern for literature and thought which led to the publication of the literary magazines.

During the same year the *Texas Journal of Education* was published, 1854, there was published in San Antonio *The Alamo Star,* a weekly paper which advertised itself as devoted to the information and amusement of the youth of Texas and to their advancement in literature and morality. The youth of Texas and other states were solicited to write articles for the paper, which was published every other Saturday from March 25, 1854, to January 29, 1855. Volume I, Numbers 1 and 4 and Volume II, Numbers 1 and 21 are bound together in one volume in the Texas Collection in the University of Texas Library. Written in longhand in fading ink on the title page of Volume I, Number 1 are these words: "Very rare, only copy known to be in existence." The fact that at this early date in Texas history there was a paper whose purpose was to inform, amuse, and advance in literature and morality the youth of Texas and whose subject matter included short stories, essays, literary quotations, and a humor section is further proof of the educational and literary concern of the people of Texas.

This concern is easily seen in the earliest literary magazine located, *The Texian Monthly Magazine,* first published in July, 1858, four years after the first educational journal and the first paper for youth. The editor of *The Texian Monthly Magazine,* like many of the editors who followed her, urged the people of Texas to support the magazine, but wondered whether they would. She appealed to the readers to depend upon themselves for their literature. This appeal for the support of the public by subscription and literary contribution is a part of the history of early Texas magazines that was often repeated.

Perhaps because women had more time for inspiration and missionary work and were less concerned in the financial outcome of their effort, many of the editors were women. Sixteen of the forty magazines were edited by women.

The financial problems the editor faced were difficult ones. There was indifference on the part of the public to subscribe in sufficient numbers to insure the continuance of the publication. There was also the problem of lack of advertising, enough to insure the financial success of the publication. Getting the magazine printed and distributed were other problems the editor tried to solve. In spite of the difficulties, he—or she—continued to work with inspiration and missionary zeal, and with certain objectives clearly in mind: to develop and foster literature in a state whose best known products were cattle and cactus, not literature and thought; to raise the literary level of Texas and the South so that the people could take pride in the accomplishment; and to keep alive in Texas the spirit of the South and Southern ideals. No doubt, the editor also expected to have more financial success than others had had, but making money in most cases was of secondary importance; even losing money was secondary.

The place of publication of the magazines established Dallas as the publishing center of Texas; fourteen of the magazines were published there all the time and three others part of the time. The second city in rank of magazine publication was Austin, with six magazines published there all the time and two others part of the time. San Antonio was third with five magazines. Among other cities, small towns, and villages where magazines were published are Waco, Galveston, Strawn, Kerrville, and Bandera.

The dates of the magazines do little more than indicate the periods between 1858 and 1929 when the greatest work was being done in Texas in the field of literary magazines. The most productive ten-year period was from 1900 to 1910, when there were, according to the dates of the earliest issues of the magazines examined, twelve literary magazines published. The second most productive ten-year period was from 1890 to 1900, when there were nine literary magazines published. It is also interesting to note that of the forty magazines studied only *Southwest Review* and *Frontier Times* are still published at the time of this writing.

No matter who the editor was, or where or when the magazine was published, each magazine offers today a history of the life of its time and presents a permanent record of the great effort made to create in Texas a literary culture.

The Texian Monthly Magazine

Mrs. E. Spann founded *The Texian Monthly Magazine* in Galveston in July, 1858, with some temerity. In her "Salutatory" she stated:

> ...knowing as I do, full well the disadvantages that I labor under in consequence of the many drawbracks [sic] upon a literary enterprize [sic], I have at least one point of support on which to rest. *I am not a stranger.* No wild spirit of adventure, no impulse of speculation or peculation guides me. . . . I will only promise to make my serial as good as Southern writers and Southern feelings and principles can make it.[1]

She appealed to the people of Texas and of the South in general to support the magazine and wondered if "the people instead of supporting the cheap, and too often deleterious Literature of the North" would now depend upon themselves for their literature.[2] After pointing out there was ". . . but one magazine (Russel's [sic]) of a purely Literary character published south of Richmond, Va. . . .," she declared, "Our mails are burdened with Northern publications."[3] Mrs. Spann disclaimed any intention to be political, but she admitted she could not write upon a theme of this kind without feeling, and she had much to say on the subject of whether a pure Southern literature could be supported.[4]

The magazine was, according to the description following the title on the cover, "Devoted to Literature, Historical Romance, Original Tales, Incidents in the History of Texas, and Selections from the Most Approved and Popular Authors." Also on the cover were these words: "All Communications on business connected with this Work must be addressed to the Editress."

The contents of Volume I, Number 1, July, 1858, as listed on the back of the cover, include, in addition to the Introduction and Salutatory: the first chapters of a French novel, French biogra-

---

1. *The Texian Monthly Magazine*, I, No. 1 (July, 1858), 3.
2. *Ibid.*
3. *Russell's Magazine*, published April, 1857, to March, 1860, in Charleston, edited by Paul Hamilton Hayne.
4. *The Texian Monthly Magazine*, I, No. 1 (July, 1858), 4.

phy, and French historical romance respectively—all translated by Mrs. Spann; three poems (one, covering three and one-half pages, was written for the magazine by Ebenezer Allen); a speech of the Hon. John H. Reagan on the death of General Rusk and a speech of the Hon. Guy M. Bryan on the death of Gen. Henderson—both delivered before the United States House of Representatives; an essay entitled "A Photograph of the United States Senate of 1858"; and articles entitled "Heroes of the Revolution" (taken from the *New Hampshire Patriot*) and "Distinguished Dead of 1857" (taken from the *New York Tablet*).

Between pages 2 and 3, on a small, yellow inserted sheet carrying the title "Notices of the Press," are two complimentary quotations about the magazine: one from the *New Orleans Catholic Standard*, the other from the *San Antonio Ledger*.

Volume I, Number 3, September, 1858, carries the third chapters of the French novel, biography, and historical romance respectively (again translated from the French by the editor), as well as other works in keeping with its purpose.

Volume I, Numbers 1 and 3 were the only two copies of *The Texian Monthly Magazine* that could be located. Both are in the Texas Collection of the University of Texas Library.

Title: *The Texian Monthly Magazine.*
First issue: July, 1858. Last issue located: September, 1858.
Periodicity: Monthly.
Editor: Mrs. E. Spann.
Publisher: Cherry, Dunn and Company, Printers, Galveston.
Size: 23.5 cm. Pages: 80.
Price: Three dollars per year.

Allan's Texas Monthly

Printed on the cover of this early Texas magazine was the following:

> Please let this lie in a conspicuous place where all may read it. Allan's Texas Monthly Vol. I No. 1 June 1867 "A Magazine of Miscellaneous Selections and Live Advertisements." The Art of advertising consists chiefly in putting business before the public in such a manner that it will be novel and attractive.

The plan of the editor was given in the preface on the first page as follows:

> This No. of *Allan's Texas Monthly* is hardly a fair specimen of what we intend making it, excepting in the typographical execution. This, thanks to Messrs. Gray, Smallwood & Co., will compare favorably with similar work anywhere. The *object* of the Magazine shows for itself plainly— "the putting of advertisements before dealers and consumers in a manner that must *attract* their attention." In this we think we have succeeded. We believe our "Miscellaneous Selections" will be found interesting enough to admit our Magazine to the home-circle. We promise greater variety hereafter.[5]

Besides the preface, the contents included a discussion of the "Houston Board of Trade"; a description of a "Thrilling Adventure" with Australian Bushrangers; "Ancestral Dispute," a quotation from the *Quarterly Review;* a story entitled "Obadiah Leatherly"; a short essay on the "Folly of Anticipating Trouble"; "Dies Irae," a poem by Henry J. Macdonald; a short allegory, "The Giant and the Dwarf"; a short paragraph, "Kiss Cotillion"; "Daniel O'Rourke," a short story; an essay on advertising under the title "What Is Worth Doing, etc."; and "Brick Pomeroy," a short paragraph.

The make-up of the magazine was unusual. The right-hand pages were divided into four sections filled with advertising; the left-hand pages were filled with the printed matter listed in the table of contents.

---

5. *Allan's Texas Monthly*, I, No. 1 (June, 1867), 1.

Two copies of *Allan's Texas Monthly* were located. One copy is in the Rare Books Room in the Library of Congress; the other in the Texas Collection of the University of Texas Library. Both copies are of Volume I, Number 1, June, 1867.

Title: *Allan's Texas Monthly: A Free Magazine of Miscellaneous Selections.*
First issue: June, 1867, the only issue located.
Periodicity: Monthly.
Editor: Harry L. Allan.
Publisher: Harry L. Allan, Houston.
Size: 22½ cm. Pages: 80.
Price: Free.

The Stylus

On the cover of the Volume I, Number 1, February, 1876, issue of *The Stylus: A Monthly Magazine Devoted To Literature, Science and Art* in the University of Texas Library are these words, written in longhand: "This complete series 1-5 incl. was presented to me by my Friend Horace Rowe, Editor, who wrote most of The Stylus." The note is signed by Swante Palm.[6] On the inside front cover, also written in longhand by Swante Palm, is this explanation:

> This monthly adventure was started by Horace Rowe, a native product of Austin, well known in town where he grew up. He inherited some property, land and valuables, after his father, Doctor Rowe, who was once speaker of the House of Rep. in the Republic of Texas. The son Horace squandered his property, wrote verse, was idle and drank some. His health failed, he went out "Ranging" 1876 and with that and probably from want of subscribers, this Stylus failed with the Fifth number. McComb I did not know.

The "Salutatory," printed on yellow paper, was inserted inside the front cover and read in part as follows:

> By an unexpected revolution of the mysterious Wheel of Chance, I find myself occupying the position of senior editor of the *Stylus*. For the past few months a periodical—the *Literary Guardian*[7]—has been published at Waco under the supervision and control of Messrs. McComb and Bagby. Upon the withdrawal of the latter gentleman from that journal, I made Mr. McComb a proposition to form a partnership with him if he would change the place of publication to Austin. He offered no demurrer....
>
> I am truly cognizant of the fact that the chance for success of a magazine of this character, published in Texas, is most uncomfortably dubious. But our State is now sufficiently developed in refinement and culture to warrant an

6. Sir Swante Palm, a native of Sweden, came to Texas when quite a young man, was postmaster at Austin for two terms, and served more than thirty years as Swedish and Norwegian vice-consul in Austin. In 1883 King Oscar of Sweden conferred upon him the honor of knighthood. In 1897 Swante Palm donated his library to The University of Texas. He died in 1899. "Sir Swante Palm," *The Alcalde*, XXI, No. 5 (February, 1933), 106-107.

7. No copies of the *Literary Guardian* could be found.

attempt at this time; and I beg that the friends of literature everywhere, whether in Texas or in sister States, will not disdain to peruse a few pages of the *Stylus* before they pronounce an anathema against its merits.

The first number contained the first installment of a romance, a short Christmas story, a descriptive essay, the first installment of a novel *Paul De Vere or The Fate of Sin* by Horace Rowe, three poems, "Facts and Fun," and "Editorials."

Contributions such as romances, stories, and articles relating to science and art were solicited. A liberal price was offered for any such articles the editors thought fit or suitable for the pages of the magazine.[8]

As Number 5 of Volume I was the last issue, the novel *Paul De Vere* by Horace Rowe was not concluded. On Page 192 of this issue notice was given that the editor found it necessary to suspend his labor on the magazine because of ill health. His physician had advised him to spend the next few months in Mexico. In his absence *The Stylus* was to appear each month as usual, and whatever was wonderful in Mexican politics or revolution or in the physical aspects of the country was to be gathered for the readers of *The Stylus*. By the notice is a note in pencil by Swante Palm: "Horace went a Ranging and the Stylus—ceased—."

> Title: *The Stylus: A Monthly Magazine Devoted to Literature, Science and Art.*
> First issue: February, 1876. Last issue: June, 1876.
> Periodicity: Monthly.
> Editors: Horace Rowe and W. P. McComb.
> Publishers: Horace Rowe and W. P. McComb, Austin.
> Size: 15 cm. Pages: 32.
> Price: Two dollars per year.

---

8. *The Stylus,* I, No. 1 (February, 1876), 32.

The American Sketch Book

In La Crosse, Wisconsin, in 1874, the American Sketch Book Company began publication of a magazine edited by Bella French. The magazine was announced as a monthly, but the files of the magazine in the Library of Congress show that Volume I was issued in six numbers, Volume II in three numbers, and Volume III in one number. The editor, probably because of the irregularity of publication of her magazine, saw fit to mark the magazine with only volume and number; no month was ever given. The magazine contained historical and descriptive sketches of towns and counties in Wisconsin, together with stories, poems, and miscellaneous matter. No more issues were published in Wisconsin after Volume III, Number 1, 1876.

But under the same title, publication was continued by Bella French in Austin in 1878. The first number published in Texas was Volume IV, Number 1. The "mission" of the magazine was given on the editorial page as being

> ... not only to collect histories of different localities, and reminiscences of old times in Texas, but to give sketches and incidents of later days, together with truthful descriptions of various portions of the State, regarding their business facilities, healthfulness, location, etc. . . . The *Sketch Book*, however, will be confined to no one locality.[9]

During the same year, 1878, Bella French married Col. J. M. Swisher of Austin. Writing of her marriage in the magazine, Mrs. Swisher said:

> If any apology is necessary to our readers for our taking a male partner, we will say that we found it entirely impossible to run the *Sketch Book* without the assistance of an old settler who would set us right about names, dates, etc. when giving historical sketches in the work. . . .[10]

Because of the numerous delays occasioned by the editor's being unable to get the printing done on time, only six numbers of *The American Sketch Book* were issued in each of Volumes IV (1878-1879), V (1879-1880), and VI (1880-1881). These numbers were not issued regularly but whenever the editor could

9. *The American Sketch Book*, IV, No. 1 (1878), 65.
10. *Ibid.*, No. 4 (1878), p. 258.

get the printing done. The idea of the magazine's being issued monthly was finally abandoned. In 1882 the editor issued this statement:

> We have had a great deal of trouble and delay in getting out this issue of the *Sketch Book,* and are much later with it than we expected. In fact, we have never pretended to issue it exactly as a monthly, but as a magazine of numbers; six numbers completing a volume....
>
> ...We hope in time to issue not only a monthly, but a weekly publication. Yet up to the present time we have found it impossible to issue even every month....[11]

The trouble and delay in issuing the magazine continued; in Volume VII, Number 3, the announcement was made that it had been impossible to get the printing done in Austin. The editor stated that the office of publications would be moved if necessary, but that the magazine would be printed and there would be no more three-months' waiting to get it printed.[12] Printing was not the only difficulty. In a paragraph "What Ails the Mails" the editor presented another problem she faced: "If postmasters and mail agents want the *Sketch Book* why do they not subscribe for it, and not steal it from people who do pay for it?"[13]

In Volume VII, Number 4, it was announced that the *Sketch Book* would be issued as a quarterly.[14] Publishing even at this interval was probably impossible, since no later issues have been located.

The Table of Contents for Volume IV, Number 1, is typical: "Austin, Texas," a poem; "The Colorado," a poem by Marietta Holly; "Historical Sketch of Austin, Texas"; "Mount Bonnell," a poem by Bella French; "The Curse of the Cardigans," a story by Sarah D. Hobart; "A Reminiscence of the Late War-Letters Written by A Union Soldier to A Friend of the North"; "The Twin Sisters," a sketch about two pieces of artillery; "The Texas Poetess," a sketch; "Farm Notes"; "Scientific Notes"; "Fashion Notes"; "A Remembrance of Henry Clay," a sketch by the editor; "Jottings," short paragraphs about various subjects; "Editorials"; and "Worth Remembering," recipes.

The following criticism was quoted in Volume VI, Number 5 from *The Worcester* (Massachusetts) *Monthly Visitor,* a journal

---

11. *Ibid.,* VI, No. 1 (1880), 82.
12. *Ibid.,* VII, No. 3 (1882), 225.
13. *Ibid.,* VI, No. 3 (1880), 242.
14. *Ibid.,* VII, No. 4 (1883), 303.

which Bella French Swisher called "a first class literary and educational journal":

The *Sketch Book* is a valuable publication. One of the most useful and interesting of the kind. It is made up of historical sketches of Texas, articles, reminiscences, essays, poetical effusions and chips on all kinds of subjects, but always containing some good, wholesome thought. . . .

The *Sketch Book* should be in every household. It is neatly printed, well edited, and about the size of the *Atlantic Monthly*. Mrs. Swisher, the editor, is undoubtedly a lady of talent, as is fully evinced in all her writings, and the able manner in which the book is edited. It is published at Austin, Texas, at three dollars per annum.[15]

Title: *The American Sketch Book: An Historical and Home Monthly*.

First issue: 1874, in Texas 1878. Last issue located: 1883.
Periodicity: Three to six issues a year.
Editor: Bella French Swisher.
Publisher: Bella French Swisher, Austin.
Size: 22½ cm. Pages: 84.
Price: One dollar and fifty cents, two dollars, three dollars per year.

---

15. *Ibid.*, p. 406.

The Amaranth

The Amaranth, whose subtitle was "An Illustrated Magazine of Literature," was published monthly in Dallas by Sam H. Dixon, the editor.

The contents for the March issue, Volume II, Number 1, 1882, the only issue located, were these: a biographical sketch and portrait of Mrs. Florence D. West; an essay entitled "The Science of the Beautiful" by Lee C. Harby; "The Rowe-Gerald Controversy" by Horace Rowe; "Bayard Taylor, a Personal Sketch" by Paul H. Hayne, presumably the Southern poet; editorials; and book reviews.

In 1883 the following notice concerning *The Amaranth* appeared in *The American Sketch Book:* "Prof. Sam Dixon's *Amaranth* is dead, so the papers say. It seems that the Texas northers were too much for it. They are sometimes very hard on green things."[16] From this reference and the date of Volume II, it is reasonable to assume that *The Amaranth* was published first in 1881 and last in 1883.

This magazine of fifty-two pages, published on a good grade of paper and bound in a plain cover, was attractive. And the fact that at least one issue carried an article by Paul Hamilton Hayne shows *The Amaranth* deserved some claim to its subtitle "An Illustrated Magazine of Literature."

> Title: *The Amaranth: An Illustrated Magazine of Literature.*
> First issue located: March, 1882, the only issue located.
> Periodicity: Monthly.
> Editor: Sam H. Dixon.
> Publisher: Sam H. Dixon, Dallas.
> Size: 17½ cm. Pages: 52.
> Price: Two dollars per year.

---

16. *The American Sketch Book,* VII, No. 4 (1883), 305.

The Prairie Flower

The "editress" of *The Prairie Flower: A Literary Monthly Devoted to the Pure, the True, the Beautiful* was Mrs. C. M. Winkler. The first issue of the magazine appeared in July, 1882. The magazine was bound in either a very light yellow or light blue thin paper. The cover design was at first a burning lamp on a book, later a full-blown rose, and still later a bunch of seven pansies.

The following is a part of the "Prospectus" as it appeared on the back of the title page of Volume I, Number 1, July, 1882:

> The publication of *The Prairie Flower*, a magazine devoted to the Pure, the True, the Beautiful, is an enterprise which will begin with the July number.
>
> We propose a periodical of 32 Octavo pages first, and if we meet with encouragement, will enlarge to 48 pages, consisting of stories, poems, original and selected, a historical department, and a department for household receipts, interspersed with anecdotes, items of current events, etc.
>
> We expect to devote every energy to this work, and will endeavor to make it interesting to all classes of readers, and a first class publication.
>
> We have undertaken this alone, but believe if we have the co-operation of our friends, as there is a wide field in Texas for such a periodical, we will meet with success. All we ask is a trial.
>
> Thousands of dollars are annually sent out of the State for literature, and we believe our people will not fail to encourage home enterprise. . . .
>
> Mrs. C. M. Winkler

In the "Salutatory" the editress proposed among other things to make *The Prairie Flower* "in every respect, a first-class periodical, devoted to the dissemination of the divine principles which lie in every human breast, purity, truth, and beauty."[17]

Besides the continued stories, short stories, poems, essays, current events, historical sketches, Masonic notes, recipes, and advertisements, the magazine made a great effort to live up to its

---

17. *The Prairie Flower*, I, No. 1 (July, 1882), 29.

subtitle by including articles written especially for *The Prairie Flower*. One of these articles was by T. D. Crawford on "Influence of the Greek Drama."[18] There also appeared a series of "Letters to Young Ladies" which pointed out the evils of gossip[19] or whispering in public.[20]

Mrs. Winkler's gallant fight to bring "the Pure, the True, the Beautiful" into the life of the state lies recorded today only in the broken three-year file which has been preserved.

Title: *The Prairie Flower: A Literary Monthly Devoted to the Pure, the True, the Beautiful. Texas Prairie Flower.*
First issue: July, 1882. Last issue located: June, 1885.
Periodicity: Monthly.
Editor: Mrs. C. M. Winkler.
Publisher: Mrs. C. M. Winkler, Corsicana.
Size: 16 cm. Pages: 32.
Price: Two dollars per year.

---

18. *Ibid.*, No. 7 (January, 1883), pp. 205-207.
19. *Ibid.*, III, No. 4 (October, 1884), 831.
20. *Ibid.*, No. 9 (March, 1885), pp. 1069-1070.

The Guardian and Young Texan

The Guardian and Young Texan: A Monthly Journal Devoted to Literature and Texas Education was published in Waco. Volume I, Number 9, the only issue located, was called "New Series" and dated October, 1884. H. A. Ivy was listed as Editor and Proprietor and Dr. R. C. Burleson, President of Baylor University, as Historical Editor.

The advertisement for Baylor University made up the lower fourth of the cover. The contents included an editorial section; an article on reading; a discussion of "Waco—The Athens of the Empire State"; "A Teachers' Department" containing an article on "Reading"; a section called "Books and Periodicals"; a department "Young Texan Self-Improvement Club," made up of a lesson on the "History of the Foundation of American Government"; a page devoted to Baylor University, its work and activities; and a pseudonymous parody by "Adolescence" on "The Bells."

The magazine contained twelve pages bound in pink thin paper. The subscription price was one dollar per year.

> Title: *The Guardian and Young Texan: A Monthly Journal Devoted to Literature and Texas Education.*
> First issue located: October, 1884, the only issue located.
> Periodicity: Monthly.
> Editor: H. A. Ivy.
> Publisher: H. A. Ivy, Waco.
> Size: 21½ cm. Pages: 12.
> Price: One dollar per year.

The Lone Star Magazine

Sometime in 1886 Mrs. Lou S. Bedford began editing and publishing in Dallas *The Lone Star Magazine*. The two copies that could be located are Volume I, Number 5, March, 1887, and Volume I, Number 6, April, 1887. In addition to the title, volume, and number, the cover of both issues carries these words:

> The Press, her crown and sceptre now all radiantly
>   impearled
> With jewels of all nations in subjection holds the
>   world.

A part of the history of the magazine is in a printed insert in the April issue:

> We send you this number of *Lone Star Magazine* trusting you will read it carefully with a view to becoming a subscriber. Our design is to build up a permanent and first-class literary monthly that will keep pace with the business and educational prosperity of the State, and we need the influence of your name; and we believe, from your reputation and circumstances, that you will appreciate our effort and our work. Our magazine is increasing in popularity and circulation with each number as the letters from different parts, not only Texas, but other states, extending from Florida to Maine, fully attest. Trusting that you will give our work a favorable consideration, I remain
>
> Very Respectfully
The Editor

The contents included poems, biographical sketches, an essay, a short story, an editorial section, and literary notes.

> Title: *The Lone Star Magazine*.
> First issue located: March, 1887. Last issue located: April, 1887.
> Periodicity: Monthly.
> Editor: Mrs. Lou S. Bedford.
> Publisher: Mrs. Lou S. Bedford, Dallas.
> Size: 23 cm. Pages: 28.
> Price: One dollar and a half per year.

The Repository

The Repository was "A Magazine of Sketches and Poems, Historical and Miscellaneous, Original, Selected, Modified and Gleaned." It was "Designed To Aid In the Advancement of Thought, the Cultivation of Taste, Manners and Morality, and the Consequent Improvement of Conditions that Control Individuals, Societies and Governments."

The contents of Volume I, Number 2, the one issue located, hardly justify such an ambitious aim. They were listed as "Editorial," "Education and Genius," "Sir Walter Scott," "Selections from Scott's Poems," "Reflections," "Bird's Eye View of Texas," "The Thugs and Thuggeries of India," "The Two Ships," "Sketches by a Teacher," and "Scraps—Selected and Gleaned."

The magazine was edited and published in Austin by Mrs. E. C. Kent, who moved to Texas in January, 1871. She spent more than twenty-five years of her life teaching in the public schools of the state.[21]

Volume I, Number 1 of The Repository, according to an editorial comment in the subsequent issue, was issued in July, 1889. During August and September the editor was "sick with malaria." Writing of her illness, she said:

> Since the publication of the July number of this magazine, we have journeyed through the dark valley and lingered on the brink of the cold river. But the boatman did not come to ferry us over, so we were permitted to return to the duties of this life. . . .
>
> We have lost two months by our sickness, but our subscribers shall lose nothing. We will give them twelve numbers of the Repository for one dollar, six numbers for fifty cents.
>
> Our long illness wrought some changes in our circumstances, also in our person, intellectually and morally, as well as physically. It caused the delay of the publication of this number of the Repository. It caused us to move our sanctum. It led to a train of thoughts and reflections that do not naturally attend upon the robust in health and prosperous in business.

---

21. *The Repository*, I, No. 2 (August, September, October, 1889), 19.

Yet our spirits are buoyant with hope; but our strength and endurance are limited, and we must take care to not promise more than we can fulfill, therefore we will only say that we shall do the best we can to make this magazine interesting and instructive to all.

Cheered by the rainbow hues of hope, man goes through life triumphantly, marching boldly to the end.[22]

Nearly all the selections in the magazine were by the editor. On the back of the front cover it was stated that each number of the magazine would contain sketches and poems suitable either for declamation or reading. It was also stated that in character, style, and design *The Repository* was unlike any other magazine or paper that was then published or had been published.

Title: *The Repository: A Magazine of Sketches and Poems, Historical and Miscellaneous, Original, Selected, Modified and Gleaned.*

First issue located: August, September, October, 1889, the only issue located.

Periodicity: Monthly.

Editor: Mrs. E. C. Kent.

Publisher: Mrs. E. C. Kent, Austin.

Size: 16 cm. Pages: 10.

Price: Twelve copies, one dollar.

---

22. *Ibid.*, pp. 17-18.

The Round Table

In the introductory paragraph of the essay "Pernicious Literature," which appeared in the earliest issue of *The Round Table* that could be located (April, 1890), Curtis P. Smith indirectly described the magazine and gave its purpose:

> In glancing through the shelves of the library of a friend recently, I saw a copy of *The Round Table* side by side with a trashy dime novel. How it got there, and why I should notice such occurrences, is a mystery, but notice it I did and the striking contrast between the two publications was marked. The one an emblem of purity, the other an engine of destruction. One's mission is to elevate, the other to destroy. Both fulfill the purposes of their creation; but, how to rid our libraries of the latter, which I take for my theme, is a subject of vital interest to the reading public of America, at present time especially, as the enemies of literary reform are becoming more numerous every day. . . .
>
> The works and productions of those who seek to give us the true idea of literary excellence, should be given a hearty welcome. There are many publications, *The Round Table* included, whose manifest intention is to aid and assist each other in the glorious work of literary reform, and it is my fervent prayer that success attend their laudable efforts.[23]

To "the glorious work of literary reform" *The Round Table* was evidently devoted. A part of each issue was made up of "Club Records," papers which had been presented as programs to the different women's literary clubs in Dallas by the members on such subjects as "Historical Sketch of Constantinople" and "The Manhood of Goethe."

Volume II, Number 1, May, 1890, contained an article entitled "Facts Concerning the Seasons," which dealt with how the months came to be so named. In his essay "History Will Repeat Itself," C. P. Smith took for his theme the following: "Temporary success, and even a life time of power, attained by unscrupulous means, is a poor reward for eternity's dues." There was a description of "The Battle of Galveston," a discussion of "Heroic Features in the Character of Quentin Durward," an article entitled "Chats about Women Workers in Literary Fields," a sketch entitled "Bay-

---

23. *The Round Table*, I, No. 12 (April, 1890), 318.

lor University, Waco, Texas," a discussion of "Some Southern Writers," and twelve poems. One of the poems was Sidney Lanier's "A Ballad of Trees and the Master," but the author's name was not given; only the abbreviation "ex" followed the poem. The announcement was made that "in June we will begin the publication of a serial, *A Hero in Black* which will run through several numbers. It is a typical southern story, and the author's style well befits it."[24]

The magazine was published and edited monthly by Mrs. Sydney Smith until May, 1892, when Charles D. O'Malley became editor. The contents of the numbers of the broken files show that the editors had as their objectives to improve the literary taste of their readers and to help the South gain literary recognition.

Title: *The Round Table.*

First issue located: April, 1890. Last issue located: March, 1893.

Periodicity: Monthly.

Editors: Mrs. Sydney Smith, Charles D. O'Malley.

Publishers: Mrs. Sydney Smith, Charles D. O'Malley, Dallas.

Size: 17½ cm. Pages: 33.

Price: one dollar, two dollars per year.

24. *Ibid.*, II, No. 1 (May, 1890), 28.

The Guardian

The Guardian, "a home and family journal devoted to religion, education, and literature," was published during the nineties by S. L. Morris, in Waco, Texas. The cover was divided into two parts. Across the top of the upper part was the title. Underneath the title were three divisions. At the left was a sketch of a soldier standing at salute beside a man sitting at a table. Written above the picture were the words "The pen is mightier than the sword"; at the right was a picture of a woman rocking a baby, with another child beside the chair. Above the mother were an angel and the inscription "Angels guard thy home." Between these two pictures were the words "Devoted to Religion, Education, and Literature," and in smaller letters the words "The integrity of the home, the nation's safeguard." The bottom half of the page contained the Table of Contents.

In an article "Shall the South Have a Magazine?" by one of the editors, S. L. Morris, the purpose, plans, and a description of the magazine were given as follows:

> There can be nothing preserved in the way of authorship or polished thought without a medium. This is not the mission of the Newspaper but it is peculiarly the work of the Magazine.
>
> In the past, we have had no successful magazine peculiarly Southern. Many have started well but were soon suspended. We have therefore been obliged to depend on other sections for our authorship and best thought. Whatever may have been proper in the past we believe with many others, that we now have good sense in this country, and that we owe it to ourselves and to our children to establish and support a medium, in which we may embalm our best thought, in our homes and libraries. If not, why not?
>
> In establishing The Guardian we acted on this judgment and have done our best. . . .
>
> We use the wire staples in the manufacture of it, we have a good sermon each month, the specialty of one of our best brethren, a varied discussion of the doctrines of the Bible by our best authors. Our Bible department, and Home department are excellent, and will contain something to please and instruct every member of the home. If you have a family and have no time yourself to read it, have it in the home

for your children and friends. Bind each volume and place it in your library for future reading and reference. These volumes will enhance with each passing year. We have reached a list of 7,500 already. . . .

We pledge our best endeavors to make our magazine worthy of every home, and pleasing to every heart in the land. . . .[25]

The contents of this same issue, typical of the material published in the magazine, were as follows: "Portrait," "Sketch," "Sermon," all by John C. F. Kyger; "The Functions of Faith," "The Pearl of Great Price," and "Shall the South Have a Magazine?" by S. L. Morris; "Divine Healing" and "Mohammed Versus Christ," by James F. Duncan; "A Twisted Christian"; "Etchings for the Home: Daughters of Baylor University, Lying to Children, Definitions of Home"; a song entitled "Write Me a Letter To-Night"; "Ex-Gov. Ross' Address"; "The Faculty of Burleson College"; "Burleson College and Sketch"; and "Paragraphs."

In nearly every issue there were poems, short stories generally with a moral, and book reviews. In Volume XIV, Number 11, November, 1895, one Kate E. White, a primary teacher, reviewed "Stories of Colonial Children" by Sara L. Pratt, and Kate Douglas Wiggin's "The Birds' Christmas Carol"; but the chief concern of the magazine was religious. In the paragraph section of the same number a letter signed "A Subscriber" was quoted. One wonders how many other subscribers shared such enthusiasm for *The Guardian* and such concern for Southern literature as this:

As an old subscriber and ardent lover of Southern Journalism, I must express my great joy at the constantly increasing improvement in *The Guardian*. I sincerely wish such articles as "Thou shalt say no" and The Daughters of Baylor University could be read and re-read by every family in Texas. I feel however ashamed to say if such articles had been published in a New York or Boston Journal they would have been eagerly read by thousands. But alas, how sad it is that Southern people are so slow to appreciate Southern Journals and Southern Literature. It has occurred to me that it might be a good device for you to have *The Guardian* published in Boston. Then it would be regarded as a rare gem of literature. But I trust *The Guardian* will grow and flourish till it shall delight and gladden 10,000 Southern families, and until our whole people shall become aroused to the importance of patronizing Southern Journals and Southern Literature. These remarks are made in no jealousy

25. *The Guardian*, XIV, No. 10 (October, 1895), 388-389.

of Northern literature, for I would not detract one iota from Northern Journalism. As an American I am proud of every development of American genius and it will be a glorious day for American literature when Southern Journalism shall fill up the vast chasm and fearful want of Southern Journalism and Southern Literature.[26]

This periodical with its slight educational and literary but strong religious emphasis, was a Southern magazine with a circulation of 7,500 to 10,000—enough in itself to mark *The Guardian* as one of the most important Texas literary magazines of its time.

Title: *The Guardian.*

First issue located: January, 1891. Last issue located: December, 1895.

Periodicity: Monthly.

Editors: S. L. Morris, H. B. Morris.

Publisher: S. L. Morris, Waco.

Size: 16½-22 cm. Pages: 50.

Price: Two dollars per year.

---

26. *Ibid.*, No. 11 (November, 1895), p. 437.

The Gulf Messenger

Thrown upon her own resources after the death of her husband, Professor W. H. Foute, superintendent of Houston Public Schools, Laura E. Foute turned her attention to literature. With the cooperation of several of the leading ladies of Houston, she established the Woman's Exchange and in 1888 began the publication of *The Ladies Messenger,* the official organ of the Exchange. In 1891 Mrs. Foute visited in San Antonio and met Miss Sara Hartman. A business partnership was established; that year the magazine moved to San Antonio, ceased to be the official organ of the Exchange, and appeared under the title *The Gulf Messenger* with Miss Hartman as co-editor and publisher.

The *Houston Post,* speaking of *The Gulf Messenger,* said:

> It is a splendid publication, and bids fair to fill a field long neglected in Texas journalism. There is no reason why Texas should not have at least one creditable literary production, and the *Post* believes these brave and talented women will succeed in this field.[27]

The *Galveston Evening Tribune* also favored the appearance of a new magazine:

> *Evening Tribune* has been favored with the first number of the new literary magazine, the *Gulf Messenger.* The *Gulf Messenger* . . . is a successor to the *Ladies' Messenger,* published in Houston. From a hurried view of the contents, it may be pronounced distinctively Texas and of a high order of literature. Many of the contributors have reputations that can but add strength to the new magazine. Texas should support this magazine and make it a nucleus around which to build a literature broader than Southern.[28]

The following notice was taken from the *Boston Pilot:*

> The *Gulf Messenger* of San Antonio is an excellent literary magazine edited and published by two bright women. . . . Among its contributors are Dora R. Miller, John Sjolander, Mary Ashley Townsend, Albert Monson and the popular Boston writer, Mrs. Cora Stuart Wheeler, who con-

---

27. *The Gulf Messenger,* V, No. 2 (January, 1892), 72.
28. *Ibid.*

tributes a very readable paper on the well known artist, Henry Sandham, entitled "Side Lights in a Boston Studio." We wish the *Gulf Messenger* a long career and a big subscription list.[29]

In Volume V, Number 5, March, 1892, the "Press Notices" printed were still favorable. The following, quoted on page 144, is from *Kit's London Letter in Toronto* (Canada) *Mail:*

> The *Gulf Messenger* is a bright and charming magazine published in San Antonio, Texas. . . . It promises to be a publication of high order of literature, and as it is conducted solely by women, I think we all ought to receive it favorably. . . . Several people here in London to whom I have shown the magazine declare they did not think such good literary work was being produced "out west," and indeed anything brighter could hardly be found than the new magazine, to which we all wish a long career of success. It takes a great deal of bravery and courage to start a literary magazine in Texas, or indeed anywhere else, and when two women, alone and unaided, undertake the task they ought to and will be splendidly supported. The *Gulf Messenger* is well gotten up, the articles and stories are well written, and it is edited with extreme care.

When Mrs. Foute died in December, 1893, *The Gulf Messenger*, "Illustrated Monthly Magazine of the Gulf States," was continued by Miss Hartman as editor and proprietor.

In December, 1896, *The Gulf Messenger* was combined with *Current Topics*, which had been published for more than five years in New Orleans. In January, 1897, *The Gulf Messenger*, which was then being published in Houston, announced a new editorial policy which was in keeping with the combination just made, but was a departure from the national literary appeal policy:

> . . . the idea is to make *The Gulf Messenger* a representative of the literary and artistic merit of Texas and Louisiana. Surely rich beams of romance and poetry can be found in either state, and only proper workmen to bring them out in beautiful measure and polished sentences are needed. . . .
>
> But *The Messenger* hopes to tell of other things as well as of our glorious past—of the outside world, its movements and present interest. The current events of the days shall be noted as they pass with all their significance, and the principal events of the social world of Texas and Louisiana

---

29. *Ibid.*, p. 3.

will be chronicled. Sketches of prominent people and places of the two states will be given, and a corner will be left for the mention of new books.[30]

The Gulf Messenger and Current Topics staff was composed of Mrs. Fannie Reese Pugh, editor; and Mrs. Margaret H. Foster and Mrs. May W. Mount, associate editors.

In the February-March, 1898, issue, announcement was made of another consolidation:

> We are pleased to announce to our readers and friends that consolidation of forces has been arranged between *The Gulf Messenger* and *The Texas Magazine*. . . .[31] As is well known, *The Gulf Messenger*, now in its eleventh volume, is the oldest literary magazine of the South. Recognized from the Atlantic to the Pacific as the representative Southern magazine, and distinctively a Texas enterprise, it has devoted friends and patrons. . . .
>
> *The Texas Magazine*, a younger but very worthy aspirant in the literary field, distinctly Southern and vigorously Texas, seeks to broaden its outlook and extend its field; hence *The Texas Magazine* and *Gulf Messenger* consolidated. . . .
>
> The business management will be vested in the Texas Magazine Publishing Co. at Dallas, Texas.[32]

Further announcements were made that the magazine would be published in Dallas and that the editor of *The Gulf Messenger*, Mrs. Fannie Reese Pugh, would be associated with the new enterprise as special correspondent and as editor of the Woman's Club Department.

A typical issue as far as contents are concerned was that for August and September, 1892. This issue contained an etching of Madame Carmen Romero Ruibio Diaz, followed by a biographical sketch of the lady; Part I of a two-part article, "Three Weeks in Yellowstone National Park" by Mary McClure; a poem, "A Song To Her" by John P. Sjolander; a short story, "A Laugh For Jove" by E. E. Carnett; the conclusion of a serial "Eudora" by Robert Boggs; another poem, "A Year Ago" by Lillian Plunkett; another short story, "At a Picnic" by E. Welden; an essay, "Among the Quakers" by Mrs. Mary Riddell Corley; one section entitled "Notes, Comments and Reviews" and another entitled "Melange."

Its mechanical makeup, type of material published, comparatively long life, and the favorable comments it drew from other

---

30. *Ibid.*, X, No. 1 (January, 1897), 43-44.
31. See page 36.
32. *The Gulf Messenger*, XI, No. 2 (February-March, 1898), 89.

publishers establish *The Gulf Messenger* as an important literary magazine of Texas.

Title: *The Gulf Messenger: Illustrated Monthly Magazine of the Gulf States* (Successor to *The Ladies Messenger* established in 1888 by Laura E. Foute). Later known as *The Gulf Messenger and Current Topics.*

First issue: December, 1891. Last issue: February, March, 1898.

Periodicity: Monthly.

Editors: Laura E. Foute, Sara Hartman, Mrs. Fannie Reese Pugh.

Publisher: Texas Magazine Publishing Co., San Antonio, Houston, Dallas.

Size: 17 cm. Pages: 42.

Price: One dollar per year.

The Period–
Lee's Texas Magazine

In 1893 Olive B. Lee began in Dallas *The Period,* "a monthly Magazine of Southern and Western sentiment on the leading topics of the day, carefully culled from the prominent publications throughout the land in a strictly fair and impartial manner." According to the editor and publisher,

> *The Period* publishes as its predominant feature after the manner of those immensely popular periodicals, *Public Opinion,* the *Review of Reviews,* and *Current Literature,* carefully selected editorials from the prominent publications in the South on the leading subjects of the day. It will be the purpose of *The Period* to cull from the daily, weekly and monthly issues the current thought now agitating or interesting the general mind, with the strictest impartiality, giving each side to every question without bias or prejudice, political, religious or otherwise, so that our readers may determine for themselves the merits of the phases of a case presented. Texas is largely made up of citizens from the Southern states, and who are naturally concerned with what is occurring in their former homes, the sentiments of the people now there, and there is no way of securing the information save from the press, which could be too expensive for the general reader to pay for and consume too much time for examination. *The Period,* as stated, purposes to supply this want. It is believed that such a magazine, conducted as above outlined will be welcomed and patronized by thousands. It will be characterized by strictly business principles and methods, prompt in its issuance and up to the standard in its mechanical make-up.[33]

This announcement was followed by a "Financial" section with selections from the *Memphis Appeal-Avalanche, Atlanta Constitution, New Orleans Picayune, Texas Farmer,* and *Nashville American;* and a "Political" section with clippings from *The Ledger* (Memphis, Tennessee), *Louisville Courier-Journal, St. Louis Post-Dispatch, Birmingham Age-Herald, Denver Republican, Denver News,* and *Dallas News.* The "Sociological and General"

---

33. *The Period,* I, No. 3 (October, 1893), 90.

and "Theological" sections were likewise made up of clippings from various papers.[34]

In the October, 1898, issue attention was called to the fact

> ... that all the articles and poems in this number are contributed by *Texas writers*. The prize story by Annie Laurie Alvis would grace the pages of a *McClure, Cosmopolitan,* or any leading periodical of the country. There is talent and superior talent in the South, and *Texas* is rich in literary resources as well as along other lines. The people of the South and especially Texas should give their hearty support to *The Period* and thus enable the editor to furnish its patrons with the best productions of the day. It is our aim and ambition to enlarge and otherwise enhance the value of *The Period* and to bring out the work of Southern writers. . . .[35]

This Texas number was made up of four pages of pictures of United States ships; the prize short story "Of The Two" by Annie Laurie Alvis of Ennis, Texas, to which the quotation above refers; a poem, "Idolatry" by Josephine Puett Spoonts of Fort Worth; another short story, "Patient Robbie" by Mrs. Maggie Field of Avalon, Texas; and three other poems: "A Lover's Farewell," by Mrs. Ben M. Williams of Bowie, Texas; "My Prayer" by Clifford McKinney Taylor; and "Oh, Meet Me" by Mrs. Augusta H. Anthony. In the editorial section there were paragraphs about the magazine and an article on Canada, "Our Neighbor" by Magnus More of Toronto.

Two important announcements were made in Volume VI, Number 12, May, 1899, on the editorial page: one, that "*The Period* with this number completes its 6th year of existence. . . . It is the *only literary* magazine now regularly published in the state, having survived several ventures which were underway, or having started subsequent to *The Period's* first issue"; two, that "the name will be changed to attest more particularly the sphere it fills and is to fill, and will hereafter be called *Lee's Texas Magazine.*"

The title, however, had undergone change before. From the beginning (August, 1893) until May, 1898, the name of the magazine was *The Period*. Then the name became *The Period* with the second title, *Lee's Magazine,* added; these two names were carried on the cover from June, 1898, through May, 1899. From June, 1899, until February, 1901, the magazine was *Lee's Texas Magazine*. From February, 1901, until the last issue in December, 1906, the magazine was called *Lee's Magazine*.

---

34. *Ibid.*, pp. 90-100.
35. *Ibid.*, VI, No. 5 (October, 1898), 116.

Lee's Texas Magazine differed very little from *The Period*. There was added a "Department of Literature," edited by Tessa Willingham Roddey, in which "Representative Men of Letters," such as Richard Harding Davis, Francis Marion Crawford, Lew Wallace, and Hall Caine and their representative works were discussed. This feature appeared more or less regularly. A section called "Literary Notes," which had been a part of *The Period— Lee's Magazine*, was continued in *Lee's Texas Magazine*. Short reviews of new books were given in this section. Among the books mentioned or reviewed were *Over the Shoals* by Lelia Mary Evans, *To Have and To Hold* by Mary Johnston, and *The Fate of Madam LeTour* by Mrs. Paddock.

When the magazine began in 1893, the predominant feature was the review section made up of selected editorials from the leading publications in the South on the subjects of the day. The importance of this feature diminished, however, as the magazine became more literary. In 1898, in an editorial, the aim of the magazine was stated as being "to enlarge and otherwise enhance the value of *The Period* and to bring out the work of Southern writers. . . ."[36] In May of the next year in another editorial the magazine was called "the *only literary magazine* now regularly published in the state."[37] The literary emphasis was maintained for as long as the magazine was published, which was until December, 1906.

> Titles: *The Period, The Period — Lee's Magazine, Lee's Texas Magazine, Lee's Magazine.*
> First issue: August, 1893. Last issue: November, December, 1906.
> Periodicity: Monthly.
> Editor: Olive B. Lee.
> Publisher: Olive B. Lee, Dallas, Houston.
> Size: 16-25 cm. Pages: 32+
> Price: One dollar and a half per year. One dollar per year.

---

36. *Ibid.*, VI, No. 5 (October, 1898), 116.
37. *Ibid.*, No. 12 (May, 1899), 264.

The New South

In the fall of 1894 R. R. Gilbert began in Galveston a "non-sectarian and non-partisan literary magazine, devoted to the interests of the Southern states." Its title was *The New South.* For three months the old South was compared with the new. But with Volume I, Number 4, January, 1895, notice was given that the magazine would be published in the future strictly as an *Immigration Journal.* The reason for the change of policy, according to a statement by the editor in the only copy of this publication located, was that as the attention of the entire Northwest had at last been turned toward Texas and as thousands were making preparations to become citizens of Texas, the time had come to make known to immigrants the inducements Texas had to offer. To make these inducements known, *The New South* proposed this:

> Employ some one in your county to write it up and show its natural and acquired resources, and say what inducements you have to offer immigrants. Then have this "write-up" verified by your county officers; then send it to *The New South....*[38]

The announcement is followed by this direct "Word of Caution":

> In giving a description of your county and its resources be candid—and you will be true to yourselves. Don't exaggerate in your own favor. Be truthful, and if your county has any great drawback, be sure and mention it, for honesty is the best policy every time....[39]

On the cover of the issue there is a pen and ink drawing of R. R. Gilbert, the editor. Underneath the drawing are the words, "Yours truly, H. P. Born in 1820." H. P. was the abbreviation for "High Private," the editor's pen name.

Most of the articles in the magazine were written by the editor. These articles include one on immigration, under the title "They Are Coming, Father Abraham." In another the author discussed the falsity of the statement that all men are born free and equal. In a serious article, boys and young men of the South

---

38. *The New South,* I, No. 4 (January, 1895), 94.
39. *Ibid.,* p. 95.

were given two points of practical business advice: (1) Choose proper associates, and (2) Maintain independence. For humor, "High Private" compared men with fishes in "A Chapter on Fishes," and in one of "High Private's Confederate Letters," he discussed "Jonah and His Whale." A long letter from S. W. S. Duncan of Dallas to the President of the Chamber of Commerce, Galveston, about "Deep Water in Texas"; a description of "The City of Alvin"; and a page and a half of short paragraphs under the heading "Salmagundi" complete the issue.

Although "High Private's" *New South* carries the subtitle "A Monthly Literary Magazine Devoted to the Interests of the Southern States," it should perhaps be classed not as a literary magazine, but as an advertising journal.

> Title: *The New South: A Monthly Literary Magazine Devoted to the Interests of the Southern States.*
> First issue located: January, 1895, the only issue located.
> Periodicity: Monthly.
> Editor: R. R. Gilbert.
> Publisher: Knapp Bros., Galveston:
> Size: 15½ cm. Pages: 32.
> Price: Two dollars per year.

The Texas Magazine

The Texas Magazine was edited and published in Austin from May, 1896 (Volume I, Number 1) to June, 1897 (Volume II, Number 14) by Robert E. McCleary. In the latter issue this announcement was made by McCleary:

> *The Texas Magazine* has been sold to Mr. Wm. G. Scarff, and will hereafter be published at Dallas. He will complete all unexpired subscriptions....[40]

The July, 1897, issue was numbered Volume III, Number 1. The editorial announcement was three pages in length; a part of it is as follows:

> The regular department for original contributions to the Magazine will be kept up to the highest standard of excellence possible, and the outlook for the coming year promises some very valuable and readable papers. The "Life of Santa Anna" by C. W. Raines, begun a year ago, will be completed; and the future chapters of that exhaustive biography will be especially entertaining, as they cover a period of the distinguished Mexican's career not heretofore generally known or understood by American readers. Among the other entertaining contributions to appear in future issues for the year, may be mentioned an account of the "War of the Regulators and Moderators," by Ex-Governor O. M. Roberts, who saw the closing events of that memorable outbreak in Eastern Texas; "Personal and Political Memoirs," by Ex-Governors Roberts and Lubbock; "Recollections of Stephen F. Austin," by Moses Austin Bryan; the "Fiscal History of the Texas Republic"; "Recollections of Old Washington on the Brazos"; "Old Anahuac and Its Memories"; Shakespearian and Critical Studies; a number of Short Stories and Anecdotal Narratives; several excellent Poems; and in short, an array of choice productions by competent authors, sufficient to assure the readers of the Magazine of a satisfactory publication for the current year.[41]

The first issue of the magazine contained the first installment of C. W. Raines's "Life of Antonio Lopez De Santa Anna"; three poems by L. R. Hamberlin; a descriptive essay on Mexico City

---

40. *The Texas Magazine*, II, No. 14 (June, 1897), 469.
41. *Ibid.*, III, No. 1 (July, 1897), 38.

by Robert E. McCleary; and a section entitled "Antiquities." The items in this section included an article from the *Ulster County Gazette*, Kingston, N. Y., published January 4, 1800, telling of the burial of George Washington; a copy of a letter from Lord Macaulay dated London, May 23, 1857, to Henry S. Randall; and the denunciation of Clay by Randolph, the words that brought about the duel between the two men.

The magazine grew larger in page size and in number of pages. The April, 1898, issue of the magazine contained a description of "Cattle Ranches and Ranchmen," by William Edgar Hughes; under "Dixie Sketches," a tale by John Sheppard Croce entitled "Sociable Tommy"; "The Romance of Berthe De Rémiguy," a "charming romance" translated for the magazine by Miss Amélie Fontant Beauregard; a historical sketch of "The Child Monarch of Spain" by W. H. Orr; a discussion of "Some of our Southern Literary Ancestors—II" by Virginia Quitman McNealus; "Shakespearean Studies," a discussion of Lady Macduff; two short stories; a poem, "From the American Flag" by Joseph Rodman Drake; a summary of the work of the Daughters of the Republic of Texas; the conclusion of the "Life of Antonio Lopez De Santa Anna" by C. W. Raines; an editorial section; a page of poetry; and a poem, "Loss or Gain?" by John P. Sjolander.

As John P. Sjolander is the same Texas poet whose poems had appeared from time to time in *The Gulf Messenger*, the manuscript for this poem may have been inherited from the defunct *Gulf Messenger*, which had been absorbed by *The Texas Magazine* the preceding month.

An insertion in the April issue to the subscribers stated:

> Owing to a reorganization of *The Texas Magazine*, two numbers, February and March, have been omitted; a regular and uninterrupted issue will begin with the April magazine. All persons holding subscriptions to *The Texas Magazine* before April 1898, will have their subscription extended two months.
>
> Texas Magazine Co.

However, *The Texas Magazine* lasted only one month after it was merged with *The Gulf Messenger* and reorganized, for the April, 1898, issue (Volume IV, Number 2) was the last number published.[42]

This magazine is not in the Rare Books Room at the Library of Congress, but it is in the Rare Books Collection of the Texas Col-

---

42. Information from card catalogue, Library of Congress, Washington, D. C.

lection at The University of Texas. Perhaps Raines's "Life of Santa Anna," which was first published in the magazine, is enough in itself to justify the classification of *The Texas Magazine* as a rare book and one of the most important of Texas magazines.

Title: *The Texas Magazine: The Texas Monthly Magazine.*

First issue: May, 1896. Last issue: April, 1899.

Periodicity: Monthly.

Editors: Robert E. McCleary, W. C. Scarff, and others.

Publishers: Robert E. McCleary, Austin; W. C. Scarff, Texas Magazine Company, Dallas.

Size: 23-25 cm. Pages: 32-58.

Price: One dollar per year. One dollar and a half per year.

Southern Home Magazine

H. P. Simonds, editor and publisher of the *Southern Home Magazine,* in the "Publisher's Department" of the May, 1897, issue, made the following announcements concerning his magazine:

> The *Southern Home Magazine* is established to earn a livelihood for the publisher. I expect to make it as good a magazine as limited capital and ability will permit. I will illustrate as fully as possible. The style of literature will be pure and not trashy. Nothing will be printed that is unworthy to go into the home. I expect to improve it and have arrangements made to publish a good magazine, one which Sherman people ought to support. I believe a magazine, with a general circulation will advance the interests of Sherman by advertising its schools which are the pride of the city.
>
> Very truly,
H. P. Simonds
>
> The *Southern Home Magazine* is the successor to *Southern Sunshine,*[43] published some years ago at Cleburne. We have taken our old number and the next number will be Volume III, Number 1.[44]

The May, 1897, number was approximately one hundred pages. On the cover was a picture of the first Confederate Monument in Texas, which was erected at Sherman, April 3, 1896. The first article was one on the monument, telling of "its history from its inception, how the monument was started, and its final result, with description of the shaft." There were three short stories: "Billy Billson's Fire" by Winthrop Packard, "On the San Pedro Trail" by Stewart Lawrence, and "Williams of Rhode Island" by Frank H. Sweet. Two articles, one on the Nashville Centennial and the other on the leading survivors of the Confederacy, were reproduced by permission of the *National Magazine* published in Boston, having appeared in the March issue which they had styled their "Southern Number." The "Sketch Album" contained sketches of forty-two prominent men and one prominent woman

---

43. No issues of *Southern Sunshine* could be located.
44. *Southern Home Magazine,* II, No. 6 (May, 1897), 517.

in Texas. In the advertising section there was a full-page announcement concerning the magazine for June. It was stated that the magazine would contain

A full page photo engraving of Hon. J. W. Bailey, Member of Congress from this District. A story of absorbing interest, based on happenings in this city some years back. The events were dramatic in character, and the incidents well known to many Sherman people. The story will be contributed by a writer who is well fitted for dealing with the situation. The story will be illustrated, the drawing being done by C. B. Rogers, of the *Southern Home Magazine*. Other interesting matter to the extent of 80 pages, illustrated, will be in this issue. The price of the *Southern Magazine* is $1.00 per year; 10 cents per copy.

The November, 1897, issue, the second issue located, was printed in Dallas. The editor stated in this issue: "We have moved from Sherman, the Athens of the South, to Dallas, the Metropolis of Texas, in order to secure a better advertising field. Advertising is the very life blood of a paper. At Dallas we believe we can secure it."[45] The magazine this month was smaller, only thirty pages.

The editor, H. P. Simonds, did for a time, at least, secure in Dallas the advertising he desired. Early the next year (March, 1898), he published Volume IV, Number 2, an issue of 104 pages with many illustrations. *Southern Home Magazine* is a typical example of many early literary magazines in Texas, magazines with a variety of subject matter distinctly Southern in nature, edited by a person determined to advance Southern letters.

Title: *Southern Home Magazine*.
First issue located: May, 1897. Last issue located: March, 1898.
Periodicity: Monthly.
Editor: H. P. Simonds.
Publisher: H. P. Simonds, Sherman, Dallas.
Size: 23-25 cm. Pages: 30-104.
Price: One dollar per year.

---

45. *Ibid.*, III, No. 4 (November, 1897), 205.

The Southern Home Journal

The Southern Home Journal: A Religious, Literary, Scientific and Educational Monthly, Published in the Interest of Education, Etc., was, according to Volume II, Number 1 (the one issue that could be located), edited by W. Frances Lane and published in Dallas in May, 1898.

The title of the magazine was printed in large letters on the cover. On the back of the cover page were two long poems. The other subject matter included two short stories; essays entitled "Is Marriage a Failure?", "Moulding the Face" (on making casts), "How To Choose a Wife," "The Cuban Junta"; two pages of poetry; and a section "For Women and Home" (styles) and another "For Boy and Girls."

> Title: *The Southern Home Journal: A Religious, Literary, Scientific and Educational Monthly, Published in the Interest of Education, Etc.*
> First issue located: May, 1898, the only issue located.
> Periodicity: Monthly.
> Editor: W. Frances Lane.
> Publisher: Lane Printing Company, Dallas.
> Size: 39 cm. Pages: 16.
> Price: One dollar per year.

The Bohemian

The first step toward the publication of the magazine *The Bohemian,* edited and published by "Our Literary Club in Bohemia" and issued quarterly at Fort Worth, was the organization of a club on April 12, 1898. The object of the club was self-improvement, mutual benefit, the development of Southern literature, and eventually the giving to the public of "the fruits of our pens" in the form of a Southern magazine.[46]

The following explanation of the club's name was given by one historian: "Bohemians, as a rule, are amateur or itinerant artists in belle-lettres, paintings, music, and kindred themes of some elevation. Bohemian, as applied to literature, signifies a lack of wealth; so when you say one is a Bohemian, you mean one who excels in letters, but not in this world's goods."[47]

During the summer of 1899 the decision to launch the magazine was made. In November, 1899, appeared Volume I, Number 1. The magazine was published regularly each quarter through Volume IV, Number 4, 1903-1904. Volume V, Number 1, was not issued until the spring of 1907. This suspension of publication of the magazine was due to a serious accident which the editor-in-chief, Mrs. H. C. L. Gorman, suffered.[48]

However, the editor was not the only important figure connected with the magazine. In the World's Fair Edition this tribute was paid the husband of the editor, A. S. Gorman:

> But honor *all* honor should be given to the *power* behind the "Founder, Editor and Proprietor"—who has made it possible for four long years to issue to the public this beautiful book; for, sad to say, the "income" of dollars and cents has never paid for the making of this lovely magazine. That "power" can be recognized in the picture of the husband of "the founder, etc." for had it not been for his generosity, *The Bohemian* would have found a grave three years ago— so to him let all the praise be given.[49]

---

46. "The Story of *The Bohemian*" (World's Fair Edition, Souvenir Number, 1904), p. 181.

47. *Ibid.*

48. *The Bohemian,* V, No. 1 (Spring, 1907), 2.

49. "The Story of *The Bohemian*" (World's Fair Edition, Souvenir Number, 1904), p. 181.

Henrie Clay Ligon Gorman and her husband, A. S. Gorman, were both from Georgia. They were married in 1870 and moved to Fort Worth in 1876.[50] These two persons took pride in their work. The editor spoke of the magazine as "beautiful and attractive" and "the first and only first class literary magazine in the South."[51] It was a pretty and prosperous-looking magazine, with its purple and yellow printing on the cover, its good grade of paper, its hundred pages, and an imposing table of contents which usually contained these main divisions: "Our Portrait Gallery," "Historical Gleanings," "With the Poets," "Facts and Fictions," "Music," "Lessons on Health," "Fraternity," "Temperance and Bible Stories," "Hints for the Toilet," "In the Dining Room," "Educational, Elocution, and Drama Sketches," "Essays," and "Our Boys and Girls." Contributors, of course, were nearly always Texans, and frequently members of "Our Literary Club in Bohemia." There were, however, some contributors who lived and worked outside the Texas border; among the most important of these were Will Allen Dromgoole of Estill Springs, Tennessee, and Samuel Minturn Peck, whose address was given as New York City.

> Title: *The Bohemian.*
> First issue: November, 1899. Last issue: Fall, 1907.
> Periodicity: Quarterly.
> Editor: Mrs. Henrie Clay Ligon Gorman.
> Publishers: Our Literary Club in Bohemia, Fort Worth.
> Size: 25½ cm. Pages: 100-113.
> Price: One dollar per year.

---

50. *The Bohemian,* V, No. 1 (Spring, 1907), 186.
51. *Ibid.,* p. 2.

Corona

Mrs. Bendetta Moore Tobin of Austin began the work of establishing the magazine *Corona* in the fall of 1900. In April, 1901, she died. However, the first issue of the magazine was published in August, 1901, at Dallas. It carried a notice of her death, and her plans for the magazine were discussed briefly.[52]

The "Announcement," or salutation, of the publisher given in the first number was almost a page in length. A part of it reads as follows:

> A new enterprise to be worthy of public consideration must have an abiding purpose, a well defined aim, and a thorough appreciation of the demands of those to whom it addresses itself. *Corona* will be published monthly. It will seek to amuse, entertain, instruct and elevate. Character sketches, biographical notes, short stories, miscellaneous matter, current events, poetry and in fact, all that touches the life and interest of women will constitute its offering. It will give special attention to the organizations which are promoted and supported by women.
>
> ... *Corona* asks no higher function than to become, in a measure at least, an inspiration to greater and nobler achievement. ... [53]

On the first page also were the following four lines by Joaquin Miller under the title "Texas":

> Above, above such skies of blue,
> Below, below such flower-sown sod,
> While ever and ever between the two,
> Go the wonderful works of God.

There were six other poems in the magazine and a full page of selected verse. Among the prose selections were articles with such titles as "Famous Songs of a Century," "Mirabeau Bonaparte Lamar," and "Religion and Philanthropy." The paper and print were of high quality. Page after page was devoted to "Prominent Women and Men of Texas" of San Antonio, Cuero, Houston, Dallas, Galveston, and Beaumont. These pages contained biographical sketches and half tones. Special attention was given to wom-

---

52. *Corona*, I, No. 1 (August, 1901), 2.
53. *Ibid.*, p. 1.

en important in the work of the Daughters of the Confederacy, Daughters of the Republic, and the Colonial Dames.

Title: *Corona: An Illustrated Monthly Magazine.*
First issue: August, 1901, the only issue located.
Periodicity: Monthly.
Editor: Not given.
Publisher: Texas Historical Publishing Company, Dallas.
Size: 24 cm. Pages: 38.
Price: Three dollars per year.

Major's Magazine

Major's Magazine: An Illustrated Southern Monthly, was published in Dallas by Alex H. Major.

The Confederate Reunion Number (Volume III, Number 7, April, 1902), the only one located, was bound in heavy white paper. The cover bore the title and the subtitle and a picture of a Southern soldier carrying the Confederate flag. The issue was filled with many photographs of Southern women. In an essay, "Preservers of the Ideal," A. F. Grubbs took as his theme that the true soul of the Confederacy lives in the hearts of Southern women. "The Immaculate Man" was the subject of an essay by S. Isabel Dickson, in which she discussed the true feeling of women in regard to love of God and home. Lela Fisher Woodward in another essay wrote of "The Mocking-Bird—Herald of Spring in the South." Besides these essays, the number contained two illustrated short stories, an illustrated poem by Maude F. Hymers entitled "The Blue and the Gray," and a critical review of current attractions on the stage.

All the other numbers might not have been so marked in their Southern theme as this one, but judging by the only issue examined, the editor was fully aware of the word *Southern* in the subtitle of the magazine.

> Title: *Major's Magazines An Illustrated Southern Monthly.*
> First issue located: April, 1902, the only issue located.
> Periodicity: Monthly.
> Editor: Alex H. Major.
> Publisher: Alex H. Major, Dallas.
> Size: 26½ cm. Pages: 62.
> Price: One dollar per year.

Dixieland

Dixieland: The Illustrated Home Magazine of the South was devoted to Southern life and literature, and dedicated to those who had died for the Confederacy.

According to the editor, its appeal was due to these characteristics: it was strictly Southern in its style and sentiment; it brought before the present generation the same loyal feeling that existed in the lives and hearts of their predecessors; in addition to interest and pleasure, it offered instruction and education to its readers; in it there were departments of interest to everyone, whether in business, educational, or home affairs; it had only the very best Southern writers on its editorial staff; and it especially appealed to those who had worn the gray and to their children because, through its columns, it brought back memories of events and occurrences dear to the hearts of all.[54]

The March number was announced as follows in the February issue:

> A half-tone portrait of Hon. John H. Reagan, the Grand Old Man of the Southern Confederacy, will appear on the *Dixieland* cover, and "Southern Lights in History" will contain a sketch of his eventful life. The Vanderbilt University will be the feature of the Educational Department.
>
> Lovers of Art will be charmed with beautifully illustrated articles on "The Annunciation in the Art of Renaissance." Another interesting article on "Nature Study" is from the pen of Miss Ellie Steele, so widely known through her botanical articles, especially her contribution to Munsey, "The Texas Blue Bonnet" which has been extensively copied by Eastern magazines. A feature of especial interest to veterans will be a sketch and full portrait of General Clement A. Evans, the gallant commander of the Tennessee Department U. C. V.
>
> Camp and Chapter and all the other Departments of *Dixieland* (Writers and Books, Fashion Notes, Music, Little Friends of Dixieland) will be replete with interest. Clever verse and fiction will also find place in its pages, and it may

---

54. *Dixieland*, I, No. 2 (February, 1904), 3.

confidently be expected that the March number will far exceed the preceding ones.[55]

The first number of *Dixieland* (not located) was published in Dallas in January, 1904. Mrs. May Guillot Potter was managing editor and Vivian Louise Aunspaugh was art editor. The editorial staff was later increased and changed to include, besides Mrs. Potter as managing editor, Floyd A. Dernier, advertising manager; Mrs. H. A. Clopton, circulation manager; and Lewis System, illustrator and designer. There was a New York office at 23 Park Row as well as the Dallas office at 262 Commerce Street.[56]

Title: *Dixieland: The Illustrated Home Magazine of the South.*
First issue located: February, 1904. Last issue located: December, 1906.
Periodicity: Monthly.
Editor: May Guillot Potter.
Publisher: Dixieland Publishing Company, Dallas.
Size: 25½ cm. Pages: 32.
Price: One dollar per year.

55. *Ibid.*, p. 11.
56. *Ibid.*, V, No. 3 (December, 1905), 53.

Harp of the West

Harp of the West: A Monthly Magazine Devoted to Religion, Music, Temperance and Literature was, according to the editor, "the kind of magazine for the home. It does not contain pictures of actresses flaunting a gay attire with their fictitious smiles and simulated cunning to allure the fancy of the youth and lead them from home and mother."[57] The editor also asserted that "aside from the helpful reading matter in *Harp of the West* the songs contained in it are worth far more than the subscription price."[58]

Included in the "helpful reading matter" of the one volume examined was an article entitled "Herbert Spencer," the theme of which was "that one so well fitted to grapple with great religious truths and divine revelations should remain willfully blind and ignorant of the purer, holier thing is a source of common regret and sorrow. What wasted opportunities in those countless hours of pain spent in trying 'To unify knowledge,' rather than teach the unity of the God-head."[59] There was a short story "Her Ministry" by the manager and editor-in-chief. The fact that "the theatre as an institution is still bad is proved by the testimonies of those who are most familiar with its working" was discussed by Rev. A. C. Dickson, D.D., in an essay "Ethics of the Theatre." There was also an article on "The Ongole Christian Herald Orphan Work" and another on "What is a Temperance Pledge." The poetry included Leigh Hunt's "Abou Ben Adhem"; "The Beggar Cat" by Ella Wheeler Wilcox; a quotation from Canto XI, 22-28 of Shelley's "The Revolt of Islam"; and two twenty-four line poems: "Fleeting Clouds," whose author was not given, and "Courage" by Clare Beatrice St. George.

The green cover bore, besides the title, volume, number, date, and price, these lines:

> Harp of the West, thy strings are tuned
> To Mother, home and heaven
> Tho' angels swept thy golden chords,
> No sweeter theme were given.

---

57. *Harp of the West,* II, No. 2 (March, 1904), 17.
58. *Ibid.,* p. 16.
59. *Ibid.,* p. 6.

The proprietor and musical editor was James A. Brown, one of the authors of a book of revival hymns called "Some Songs" and advertised in the magazine; his wife was associate editor; the manager and editor-in-chief was Mrs. Augusta Houghton Anthony.

It is difficult to tell from a study of one issue of this magazine whether its real purpose was to further "religion, music, temperance, and literature" or to advertise the musical compositions of the publisher.

Title: *Harp of the West: A Monthly Magazine Devoted to Religion, Music, Temperance and Literature.*

First issue located: March, 1904, the only issue located.

Periodicity: Monthly.

Editor: Mrs. Augusta Houghton Anthony.

Publisher: James A. Brown, Waco.

Size: 15 cm. Pages: 40.

Price: One dollar per year.

The American Home Journal

> The American Home Journal is conspicuously and de-
> servedly popular, especially in its home territory. . . . It will
> appeal to all lovers of a beautifully illustrated, well edited,
> wide awake, high-class family journal of exceptional attrac-
> tiveness. It will abound in literary and artistic surprises of
> the most delightful character. We have been referred to
> as the "queen of Southern monthlies". . . .[60]

Such was the praise which *The American Home Journal* gave
itself in the issue of December, 1904. The magazine, with its col-
ored cover, was published in Dallas. Each issue contained short
stories, poetry, and the following regular features: "Correct
Things to Know," "Sunshine," "Home," "Talks With Girls," "Latest Fashions," and "Boys and Girls."

The contents of Volume VI, Number 1 (February, 1905), were
these: a short, short story, "My Silhouette" by Benjamin Franklin
Napheys; a short story, "A Man, A Maid and A Matrimonial Paper" by Herbert S. Kendall; another short story, "Adeline" by Lizette Woodworth Reese, the poet; an article, "The Largest Me-
teor In the World" by H. M. Risley; an article by Julia D'Arey
on "The Antics of The Little Ladies' Club—A Society of Short
Women in New York Banded Themselves Together to Make
Themselves Grow a Little Taller, a Little Stouter and A Great
Deal More Imposing in Appearance. . . ."; "Prettiest Woman In
France and Her Beauty Arts" by Marian Martineau, an article;
a page of poetry, "Dream Voices of The South" by Harve P. Nel-
son; "Home" by Homer M. Price; a page of paragraphs var-
iously titled "Be Careful How You Judge," "Doing More
and Talking Less," and "The Kingdom Within"; "Talks With
Girls" by Haz Binwun, a plea for appreciation for mothers; "An
Hour in the Kitchen," a page of recipes; "Latest Fashions," de-
scriptions and illustrations of patterns that could be ordered;
"Correct Things To Know about Weddings" by Emily Holt; "Boys

---

60. *The American Home Journal*, V, No. 5 (December, 1904), 20.

and Girls," a poem and an essay for young people by W. Halleck Mansfield; an article, "Women's Legal Rights" by C. W. Starling; "Sunshine," a poem and an essay praising the good work of charity organizations, by Priscilla Prescote; "A Young Man In The Lead," biographical sketch of J. C. Phelps of Dallas; and "Fancy Work," directions for crocheting baby sacques, by Louise Salmons.

The policy of the magazine was changed with the issue of May, 1911.

> Beginning with the May issue of *The American Home Journal* the policy will be slightly changed, but not the name. While we will retain all the old features of so much interest to our old friends we feel it to the best interest of the magazine and particularly so to our old subscribers to expand our policy and broaden the scope of its usefulness as a Home Journal. To best accomplish this, the new company will try to have interesting articles for its readers regarding real estate and land conditions throughout not only the great South, Southwest, West, and Northwest; but, throughout the World.[61]

The American Home Journal, "the queen of Southern monthlies," was probably first published in 1901, for in Volume V, Number 5, December, 1904, Fred E. Johnson, who was listed as the secretary and manager, but who evidently served also as editor of the magazine, wrote on page 3: "I have been working very hard for the past three years trying to give the homes of the Southwest a magazine all would feel proud to have as a visitor every month." Then he stated that he had never before asked anything personal of the "dear reader," but he was now asking that each subscriber send the magazine as a gift to a relative or a friend in order to double the subscription list.

The contents of the June, 1915 (Volume XIV, Number 2) issue was much like the December, 1904, issue; there were two short stories, a woman's page, a fashion department, a page of humor, and six pages devoted to the Texas Equal Suffrage Association; in fact, *The American Home Journal* had become the official organ of the Dallas Equal Suffrage Association.

> Title: *The American Home Journal: A Monthly Magazine for the Home.*
> First issue located: December, 1904. Last issue: June, 1915.

---

61. *Ibid.,* XIII, No. 1 (May, 1911), 5.

Periodicity: Monthly.

Editors: Fred E. Johnson, J. Francis Warrick, Edward M. Rutledge, William J. Glynn.

Publishers: American Home Journal Company, Realty Printing Company, R. A. Glynn, Dallas.

Size: 39 cm. Pages: 20-24.

Price: One dollar per year.

The Southerner

In the first number of *The Southerner,* the editor of the magazine, Louella Styles Vincent, tells this story under the title "A Dream Come True":

> Long ago, when the world was young . . . I began to build a "Castle in the Air". . . . When my Castle had attained prodigious height I took in a partner; nearly every day for years a little blackeyed uncle and I would sit for hours . . . planning The Great Magazine which was to be mine. . . . The Magazine was to concentrate all virtues of all known periodicals, and, rejecting flaws and unloveliness, would become a prime requisite to every reader on the habitable globe. . . . I never outgrew this Castle in the Air. . . .
>
> When I was a happy young mother with head, heart and hands too full for dreaming . . . my boys took up the retarded construction of the same Air Castle. . . .
>
> Yes, some day, my dear ones and I would form a great Magazine . . . a medium for Southern literature. . . . The Magazine was far away, but as my children prattled, I imagined just how it would look . . . the clear type, the fine rough paper, the single headings, the plain cover, the wholesome pages.
>
> . . . my Magazine is here. Behold, *The Southerner!* This is the materialized Castle; not flawless as inexperience planned, not so fine as hoped and desired, not near perfection, but a brave, bright, buoyant advance toward attainment. . . .
>
> As we advance and become able to pay for brains and skill in the mechanical department, Upshur, my son, will gradually assume editorial management and leave me free to live and think and write as we both have always wished. In the meantime we will put into *The Southerner* every resource at our command with the hope and expectation of making it an absolute indispensable to every thoughtful reader in the South and to many all over the world who are interested in the advancement of Southern letters, or who may be curious about Southern culture, customs, point of view and opinions. Whoever you may be, read *The Southerner* and help us to make it really excellent.[62]

---

62. *The Southerner,* I, No. 1 (March, 1905), 57-59.

The initial number was bound in light tan heavy paper. Printed on the cover was the title, and under the title "An Exponent of Southern Ideals: A Bearer of Southern Standards: A Magazine of, for, and from the South, the price, ten cents a copy—a year one dollar." The contents of this number were a poem, "At New Year" by Louella Styles Vincent, the editor; a story, "The Late Repentance of Mrs. Mac Linn" by Field Andrews, the pen name of the editor; "Three Quatrains" by John P. Sjolander; an essay "A Plea for the Pines" by Field Andrews; a poem, "A Prayer" by Louella Styles Vincent; an essay, "The Songs My Mother Sang" by Mrs. Carey W. Styles, mother of the editor; a poem of four lines, "Raze Your Barriers" by the editor; "A Song of Peace," a poem by Jane Morton Ware; "My Haunted House," a sketch by Mrs. S. O. Adams; another poem by the editor, "To Texas Scots"; an essay "One of Our Heroes" by Katie Daffan; "Hebrews" a poem by Louis Gabriel; a paper on the South's literature by Mrs. Kate Alma Orgain; the beginning of a story called "Amethyst" by Louella Styles Vincent; Edward Coote Pinkney's poem "Serenade"; a description of "The Bystander Family" by Louis Gabriel; a section devoted to the Texas Federation of Women's Clubs; a section devoted to the United Daughters of the Confederacy; editorial comment; a book-review section, in which a novel called *Manassas* was severely criticized; and short reviews of "Partisan Rangers of the Confederate Army" by Adam R. Johnson and "Reminiscences of War and Peace" by Mrs. Roger A. Pryor.

> When the April number was in course of preparation Mrs. Vincent became violently ill with pneumonia, and for nearly three months was unable to write or correct. For a time it seemed that the editor and *The Southerner* had finished their work. . . . The matter in this issue was prepared for April, but it is dated June. . . .[63]

To this second number Louella Styles Vincent contributed three poems, two articles, and two stories.

The two volumes of *The Southerner* extant are a part of the Styles-Vincent Library presented to The University of Texas by James Upshur Vincent—who was graduated from the University in 1897—in memory of his parents (James U. Vincent and Louella Styles Vincent) and grandparents (Colonel Carey W. Styles and Fannie Jean Evans Styles). Bound inside the cover of the first issue of *The Southerner* is this typed letter from Upshur Vincent:

---

63. *Ibid.*, No. 2 (June, 1905), p. 63.

It seems to me that four numbers of *The Southerner* were published before a nervous breakdown made it impossible for my Mother to continue editing it and a financial breakdown made it impossible for me to continue publishing it. Looking back now at the remarkable adventure, it seems that even we should have known no such magazine could survive in a little Texas town; but we tried it! Mother was also the "Field Andrews" of this magazine and of many poetry and prose things published in different papers scattered from the Gulf to Canada. There is much of interest in these two numbers—including some quatrains by John P. Sjolander of Cedar Bayou, near Houston—possibly the greatest man who ever lived in Texas—Upshur Vincent.

The quatrains by John P. Sjolander referred to are:

I

Wisdom breathes the voice of peace,
  Strength is when men stand united;
Gentle speech brings love's increase,
  And, where love is, wrong is righted.

II

Brave is he whose bright blade dares
  To espouse the Right 'gainst many;
But the laurel wreath he wears,
  Who, when wrong, does not wield any.

III

Might's strong cause is quick in growth,
  That of Right is strengthened slowly;
But one fate awaits them both—
  Justice, pure, and high and holy.[64]

This poet, John P. Sjolander, was born in Sweden in 1851. Having come to Texas in 1871, he settled on a farm near Cedar Bayou about sixty miles from Houston. After 1885 his verse appeared often in newspapers and magazines not only in Texas but throughout the rest of the United States as well.[65] *The Southerner* was only one of several of the Texas magazines located that listed John P. Sjolander among the contributors.

The Southerner is especially interesting as it represents so well the dream and the effort of one woman in the field of Texas magazines to establish a medium for Southern literature. The fact that

---

64. *Ibid.*, p. 11.
65. Edwin Anderson Alderman and Joel Chandler Harris, eds., *Library of Southern Literature* (Atlanta: The Martin and Hoyt Company, 1907), XI, 4833-4835.

The Southerner lived only a short while does not make the ideal it represented less important.

Title: *The Southerner.*
First issue: March, 1905. Last issue: June, 1905.
Periodicity: Monthly.
Editor: Louella Styles Vincent.
Publisher: The Vincent Printing House, Strawn.
Size: 17 cm. Pages: 62.
Price: One dollar per year.

The South

The South was issued on the first of each month by The South Publishing Company, Dallas, Texas. The editorial staff as listed in Volume I, Number 5 (June, 1905), was as follows: I. A. F. Keiper, Mrs. M. K. Craig, John R. Allen, V. L. Aunspaugh, Virginia Adams, Jerome K. Jones, N. B. Ford. If V. L. Aunspaugh was Vivian Louise Aunspaugh, at least one of the members of this staff had been connected with another magazine published in Dallas; for Vivian Louise Aunspaugh was listed as art editor of *Dixieland* in 1904.[66]

Typical covers for the magazine carried on the upper half not only the title of the magazine with the words "Past, Present and Future" but also pictures of the United States flag and the Confederate flag in colors, or the words "Founded on the Traditions of the Old South, Devoted to the Upbuilding of the New" with a laurel spray forming the principal part of the background for the title. The lower half of the cover contained the table of contents; a drawing showing Theodore Roosevelt pointing out to a young man Texas and Dallas on the globe with these words: "President Roosevelt said: 'Texas is the Garden Spot of the Lord, Young man.' Dallas, the Metropolis of Texas, is located in the center of the garden"; or a photograph of some person or a scene.

The magazine was true to its title. For although "World Topics" was a regular feature and "Anecdotes of Famous People," "Beautiful Switzerland," "An European Tone," and "An Interpreter of Venice—H. W. Faulkner" were among the titles listed in tables of contents, titles related to the South made up the greater part of each issue. There were articles with such titles as "Historic Kentucky," "My Old Kentucky Home," "Some Southern Writers and Their Books," and "Under the Flag."

Besides "World Topics" and "Anecdotes of Famous People," other more or less regular features of the magazine were "Sister Robustus Papers" by Priscilla Dan, "Women Clubs," and "Talks for the Arm Chair." There were many photographs of people of importance, some poetry by members of the staff, some by other Texas contributors or copied, and one, two, or three pieces of fiction.

---

66. See page 47.

The South advertised itself in this way in March, 1906:

> *The South,* unlike many magazines which have been launched in this section of the country, has striven to improve each succeeding issue, always advancing but never retro-grading. Our success has been phenomenal since the first issue, and now we find that we are fully justified in giving to our readers, beginning with our next issue, a handsomely illustrated magazine of 40 pages including the cover, which will be printed in colors. . . .[67]

The next issue did contain forty pages and a cover printed in colors, but otherwise there was no great improvement in the magazine. The last issue located, published three years after the first but numbered Volume IX, Number 4, October, 1908, was much like other issues examined.

Title: *The South.*
First issue located: June, 1905. Last issue located: October, 1908.
Periodicity: Monthly.
Editors: I. A. F. Keiper, Mrs. N. B. Ford.
Publisher: The South Publishing Company, Dallas.
Size: 22½ cm. Pages: 34.
Price: Twenty-five cents, fifty cents per year.

---

67. *The South,* IV, No. 1 (March, 1906), 3.

Holland's

Frank P. Holland began publication of a magazine called *Farm and Ranch* in 1883. His son Frank P. Holland, Jr., who came into the business with him in January, 1900, conceived the idea of making a general magazine that would belong to all the people of the South and Southwest just as the *Farm and Ranch* belonged to farmers and ranchers of the same region. Frank, Jr., kept working with this idea and in 1905 took the first step toward its execution. At that time he bought *Street's Weekly* [68] in order to make his magazine more impressive by continuing it with the volume number of *Street's Weekly*. In July, 1905, the first issue of *Holland's*, "Successor to *Street's Weekly*," was published as Volume XXIV, Number 32, August, 1905.[69]

The publishers said in the first issue:

> With its first number *Holland's Magazine* greets the public without apology, trusting to its merits to win for it a high place in public esteem. In a sense it is wholly new—new in form, in matter and in general make up, though in another way it is old, for it is the successor of *Street's Weekly* established more than twenty-four years ago. *Holland's Magazine* has taken over the subscription list and good-will of *Street's Weekly* and all subscriptions will be filled out for the proportionate time. The subscription price for *Street's Weekly* was $2 per year, and *Holland's Magazine* will be only $1 per year, hence all readers of *Street's Weekly* whose subscriptions are paid one year in advance will receive *Holland's Magazine* for two years.
>
> ### NOT SECTIONAL OR LOCAL
>
> While there are many magazines, the number of really good ones is surprisingly small. We believe there is room for another, if its quality be right. We are going to supply the quality and look to our readers for the results. . . .
>
> Though published in the Southwest, and intended primarily for the Southwestern people, *Holland's Magazine*

---

68. *Street's Weekly* was an eight-sheet paper, first published in 1876. It was devoted to miscellaneous matter, designed to advertise a town or county. Because of its commercial nature, it was not included in this study.

69. Statements by Frank P. Holland, Jr., personal interview, Dallas, April, 1941.

will not be sectional or local in its contents. Its matter will be prepared along broad lines; its topics will be those of general interest. . . .

GOOD FICTION

Fiction will be a specially strong feature of *Holland's Magazine,* and the story writers include some of the best in America. . . . Each month there will be a number of strong stories, full of life and action, yet pure and clean—stories that can be read by the fireside and enjoyed in the home by each member of the family. In time we shall begin the publication of serials as well as short stories—but more of that later. . . .[70]

Other special sections would be included according to the following subjects: Readings, Floriculture, Fashion's Frills and Fancies, Culinary Affairs, For the Young Folks, Building Plans, Domestic and Building Economy, Hunting and Fishing.[71]

In the first issue there were five poems: "Life's Reward" by J. M. Lewis, "Helping Fairies" by Louisa A'hmuty Nash, "The Friends That Wear" by Roy Farrell Greene, "Leaves" by Jake H. Harrison, and "Calling the Cows" by Clara D. Gilbert. There were nine stories: "The End of a Strike" by F. N. Stratton, "The Fortune Teller" by Belle Maniates, "Sidney Crafton, Promoter" by Edgar White, "Mr. Long Distance" by W. Halleck Mansfield, "The Taking of Dolly" by Lorena M. Page, "The Black Hand" by Anna Bishard, "Chivalry of the Hills" by H. H. Hughes, "Seeing Parsifal" by Stephen Pelham, and "A Train Acquaintance" by R. F. Knapp. There were these special features: "Editorial," "Housewives in Cuba" by Mrs. E. Codinez, "Among the Wild Flowers" by Sallie E. Buchanan, "Cadet Life at the U. S. Naval Academy and Its Memories" by Walter B. Whitman, "Fashions," "Little Stories about People and Events," "Kitchen Hints," "The Real Race Suicide" by Hester Grey, "Good Health the Secret of Beauty," "Children's Pages," and "Fancy Work."

The cover of the first issue showed a framed picture of a group of people walking on stones in a stream in the woods. This was a lithograph, since at this time it was impossible to get engraving done anywhere nearer than Kansas City.[72] The next two issues carried covers done in three colors. The magazine featured covers picturing Dutch children or young people until 1918 when

---

70. *Holland's,* XXIV, No. 32 (August, 1905), 3.
71. *Ibid.*
72. Statements by Frank P. Holland, Jr., personal interview, Dallas, April, 1941.

the United States entered World War I; then the pictures became patriotic. After the War, the cover designs followed no certain theme, although in later years there was a preponderance of pictures of Southern locale.

Through the years, *Holland's* regular features included: gardening information, plans for Southern homes, interior-decoration information, recipes, fashions, information on beauty preparations and methods, feature articles on the South, scenic attractions of the South, Southern personalities, articles on health and family relationships, children's section, book reviews, exchange department for household ideas, fiction, and poetry. The fiction and poetry sections were enlarged from time to time, and both sections included the work of well-known authors.

Holland's, "The Magazine of the South," came to be widely circulated in West Virginia, Virginia, North Carolina, South Carolina, Georgia, Florida, Alabama, Mississippi, Tennessee, Kentucky, Arkansas, Louisiana, Oklahoma, Texas, and New Mexico.

According to the advertisement which the magazine carried each spring, every summer college boys who were carefully selected for their integrity, industry, and ability would visit homes and businesses in the South selling *Holland's*.

Holland's, with its wide circulation of more than half a million, deserved its subtitle, "The Magazine of the South." The contents were planned for people of the South, and the words *South* and *Southern* appeared often on and within its covers. The biographical sketch, which appeared under the title "Southern Personalities," was a regular feature. Sometimes there was a section called "Southern Kitchens." In "The Home and Garden" section there were articles on gardening in the South, fashions for the South, and house plans for the region. Regularly *Holland's* offered for sale its book *Town Building*, a part of "*Holland's* Southern Institute for Town Service," and its book *Distinctive Southern Homes*.

Its wide circulation assured financial success; and the wide variety of its contents—interesting fiction, good poems, and worthwhile articles—made it Texas's outstanding magazine.

Title: *Holland's: The Magazine of the South.*
First issue: August, 1905. Last issue: December, 1953.
Periodicity: Monthly.
Editor: Frank P. Holland, Jr.
Publisher: Texas Farm and Ranch Publishing Company, Dallas.
Size: 28 cm. Pages: 50+
Price: Fifty cents per year.

The American Woman's Home Journal

❧⊚❧

The "Salutatory" tells a part of the story of how *The American Woman's Home Journal* came to be.

> *The American Woman's Home Journal* is not a new paper, except in name. It is the *Twin Cities Magazine* with a change of form and a new name.[73]
>
> The publisher of the *Twin Cities Magazine* was Mr. R. I. E. Dunn of Dallas, Texas, a young man who started the periodical on March of last year (1905), intending it at the time for local circulation in Dallas and Fort Worth only. A great deal of interest was manifested in the pretty little magazine, and it got a nice list of subscribers. . . .
>
> In August last year Mr. Ward H. Mills, a man of considerable experience in newspaper work, acquired a proprietary interest with Mr. Dunn in the *Twin Cities Magazine* and *The American Woman's Home Journal* was conceived.
>
> In the Northern and Eastern States there are published quite a number of periodicals that, beginning in a small way, have achieved success at the publication price of ten cents a year.
>
> No similar venture had, up to this time, been undertaken in the Great Southwest, and the present publishers of *The American Woman's Home Journal* believe that a publication devoted distinctively to the interests of the woman at home and to the educational development of home matters of the mothers-to-be of this country would be welcomed at the subscription price of ten cents, that would enable even the poorest to avail themselves of the opportunity to read such literature.
>
> Accordingly preparations were begun in September to make the change with the January 1906 number. The October-November number of the *Twin Cities Magazine* contained the announcement of the change and the Christmas number the Foreword of *The American Woman's Home Journal*.[74]

---

73. No issues of the *Twin Cities Magazine* could be located.

74. *The American Woman's Home Journal*, III, No. 2 (January, 1906), 6.

The mission of the magazine was to promote higher ideals and nobler aspirations of the people, to encourage and to assist "the noble mothers, the wives and daughters in our land in the exercise of their home activities." The magazine was to treat the household, kitchen, and garden, as well as fashion, hygiene, beauty, fiction, and nonsense.[75]

Contents for the January, 1906, issue were a story, "The Result of a New Year's Visit" by Alice Louise Lee; an installment of a serial, "Eben Holden" by Irving Bacheller; "Editorials"; "Women —Incidents and Matters of Especial and General Interest"; "Our Girls—The Mothers and Housewives-to-be of American Homes"; "Latest Fashions"; "Poultry Parley"; "Kitchen and Cuisine"; and "Household."

Incomplete files make it impossible to tell whether *The American Woman's Home Journal* succeeded, or what finally happened to it.

Title: *The American Woman's Home Journal.*
First issue: January, 1906, the only issue located.
Periodicity: Monthly.
Editors: R. I. E. Dunn, Ward H. Mills.
Publishers: The Dunn-Mills Co., Dallas.
Size: 27 cm. Pages: 12.
Price: Ten cents per year.

---

75. *Ibid.*

Our Mascot

The ambitious year's program of Mrs. Jennie B. Mott for her magazine *Our Mascot* was outlined as follows in the "Prospectus":

From 144 to 192 pages of local history and special articles illustrated with photographs of people you know.

From 100 to 120 pages of strong special articles dealing with subjects of national interest, fully illustrated.

From fifty to seventy-five pages of personal sketches of prominent men and women in the world at large, illustrated with their latest photographs.

Twelve pages of cartoons, dealing in a humorous way with subjects of current interest.

Three hundred and sixty pages of good fiction, embracing from fifty to sixty of the very best short stories.

Forty-eight pages of the latest fashions, fully illustrated, and always in advance of the seasons.

Twelve pieces of music worth at least $8 if you bought it at music stores.

Twelve designs or plans, fully explained and illustrated for modern homes, at a reasonable price.

From seventy-five to 100 pages of short, crisp miscellany pertaining to the home.

Twenty-four pages of choice humor.[76]

While *Our Mascot* was first and last a home magazine, it was the editor's and proprietor's intention to reach out far beyond the borders of the state and tell the people about Texas and her wonderful resources and extend to strangers a cordial invitation to investigate the great advantages of the state. Mrs. Mott also had high literary ideals for her magazine. She wanted good literary contributors—men and women who were known in the world of letters. Writers of fiction, history, and verse as well as other artists were invited to make free use of the space in the magazine.

The motto of *Our Mascot* was "to promote the good; help others succeed; build and, by example, show others how to build; stimulate a desire for high ideals in the life literary, social, commercial and industrial."[77]

---

76. *Our Mascot,* I, No. 1 (April, 1906), 3.
77. *Ibid.,* p. 4.

Following the program as outlined in the "Prospectus," the first issue contained "Practical Points for Prospective Settlers," a two-page article by the editor, an essay on "Success and Failure"; an explanation of "Tunnelling the Mississippi River"; a section called "On the World's Stage," in which such figures as the King and Queen of Denmark and Herbert S. Hadley, Attorney-general of Missouri, were pictured and discussed; a page of cartoon comment; a biographical sketch of Miss Clara Driscoll, "the patriotic Texas girl"; a fiction section containing five short stories; a discussion of Raphael; a popular song entitled "You Won't Play Fair," words and music; four pages of fashion notes with photograph and description of gowns; a section, "In Stageland," consisting of two pages of pictures of famous actors; the "Scrap Bag"; a page of jokes; one page entitled "Home Building Department"; and four poems, including this poem by the editor:

The Alamo

Time hath dealt gently with thy walls—
But Death hath taken from our side
The few old Sentinels on whom we leaned
To hear the oft-repeated story of thy fall.
Yea, Time's unrelenting stroke hath claimed
Thy Heroes, and Companions all—
But in thy silence, sadly maimed,
A monument you stand, to mark their fall.[78]

The third issue, August, 1906, contained a photograph and sketch of the life and work of Pompeo Coppini, who, born in Italy in 1870, immigrated to the United States in 1896 and settled in New York. In 1902 he came to San Antonio and accepted the offer from the Daughters of the Confederacy to execute a monument to Confederate heroes for the State Capitol grounds. He was so delighted with the natural beauty and climate of San Antonio and the artistic atmosphere of Texas that he decided to make San Antonio his home. Besides the monument to the Confederate heroes, other public works of Mr. Coppini are to be found in the state, including the famous Terry's Texas Ranger statue.[79]

Among the short stories in this issue was one by Ella Wheeler Wilcox, "Trouble on Foley's Ranch." In "Our Scrap Bag" there was a poem, "Kissing the Rod," by James Whitcomb Riley.

The cover of the magazine bore the title *Our Mascot*, the subtitle "The Texas Magazine," a star with a picture of the Alamo in the center, the designation of Mrs. Jennie B. Mott as Editor

78. *Ibid.*, p. 1.
79. *Ibid.*, No. 3 (August, 1906), p. 5.

and Proprietor, and the month and price of the magazine.

Even though only three issues of the magazine could be located, they were enough to show that the editor had made a great effort to establish a Texas magazine important in the literary world.

Title: *Our Mascot: The Texas Magazine.*
First issue: April, 1906. Last issue located: August, 1906.
Periodicity: Monthly.
Editor: Mrs. Jennie B. Mott.
Publisher: Mrs. Jennie B. Mott, San Antonio.
Size: 17½ cm. Pages: 48-80.
Price: One dollar per year.

The Passing Show

The title of this magazine, which was first issued in November, 1906, varied. Its title from Volume I through Volume VI, Number 15, was *The Passing Show;* in Volume VI, Numbers 16 through 25, it was entitled *Mackay's Weekly;* from Volume VI, Number 26, through Volume VII, Number 39, it was called the *Southern Sentinel;* from Volume VII, Number 40, to Volume VIII, Number 6, it was called *Bohemian Scribbler.*[80] In the card catalogue in the Library of Congress it is stated that the *Bohemian Scribbler* was continued as the *International Magazine.*[81]

The Passing Show made clear to the public its policies as follows:

> It is a weekly journal designed to reflect the ebb and flow of event and opinion in San Antonio and in Texas, with reference to so much of the national movements as are felt here. Politics and matters of public interest, society, clubs, sports, the theatre, current literature, in fact the whole pageantry of life will be the matter offered up for amusement and mental pabulum to our readers.[82]

The subject matter of the first issue was arranged under these headings: "Society and Vaudeville," "In the Realm of Society," "Among the Clubs," "Sports," "Theatres," and "Current Literature." Under the heading "Theatres" were reviews of Annie Russell's performance as Puck in *Midsummer Night's Dream,* of a play based on *Parsifal,* and of "The Passing Season." Under "Current Literature" Jack London's *White Fang,* James Montgomery Flagg's humorous volume of verse *Why They Married,* Mrs. John Van Vorst's *Letters to Women in Love,* and Helen M. Winslow's *The President of Quex* were reviewed.

The contents of the magazine for March 12, 1910, then entitled *Mackay's Weekly,* were consistent with the policies of the magazine as given in Volume I, Number 1. Three articles—"Government by Commission," "A Glance at the World," and "Patriotic

---

80. Texas Collection, the University of Texas Library, information from card catalogue.

81. See page 76.

82. *The Passing Show,* I, No. 1 (November 17, 1906), 4.

Education"—had to do with "political and matters of public interest." Society and clubs were represented by two divisions in the magazine, "With Women's Clubs" and "Society Notes." And current literature was discussed under the titles "Bjornstjerne Bjornson" and "Books and Bookmen."[83]

Bohemian Scribbler, the title given to the magazine in April, 1911, was published monthly and took a more literary turn than its predecessors had taken. One issue contained eight poems, four short stories, one part of a serial, two historical sketches, a monologue, and the following special sections: "Clubs," "Children's Page," "Editorials," "Music," "Mothers' Council Department," and "Bookshelf." The thirty-seven pages of this issue, as the summary shows, were filled with subject matter that can be classified as literary.[84] The content of all the other issues of the *Bohemian Scribbler* which were located marked this magazine as more literary than either *The Passing Show* or *Mackay's Weekly* or *Southern Sentinel,* the three other magazines in this San Antonio magazine family.

Titles: *The Passing Show, Mackay's Weekly, Southern Sentinel, Bohemian Scribbler.*

First issue: November, 1906. Last issue: January, 1912.

Periodicity: Weekly, monthly.

Editors: John B. Carrington, Mrs. M. B. Fanwick, Duncan Mackay, Mrs. Gussie Scott Chaney, Johnnie A. Jones.

Publishers: Duncan Mackay, Bohemian Scribbler Co., Ltd., San Antonio.

Size: 24½-39 cm. Pages: 12-57.

Price: Three dollars per year, two dollars per year, one dollar and fifty cents per year.

---

83. *Mackay's Weekly,* VI, No. 18 (March 12, 1910).
84. *Bohemian Scribbler,* VIII, No. 3 (September-October, 1911).

The Green Book

In May, 1908, John V. Levy began the publication of a magazine called *The Green Book*. The publisher hoped to make his magazine as up-to-date and as large as the regular Eastern magazines, and to secure a circulation that would put it on a par with these magazines.[85]

In the "Prospectus" the publisher stated that *The Green Book* was published in a Texas town, by a native Texan, for Texas people and that a large number of the contributors were Texas authors. He asked the people to support the magazine, for without their support it could not be a success, and in the magazine business one law was immutable: that law was success or failure.[86]

Evidently the publisher did not receive from the people the support he sought; the magazine was published for only four months: May, June, July, and August, 1908. These four numbers are bound together in the Library of Congress with this typed letter:

Galveston, Tex.
Dec. 7, 1908

Librarian of Congress
Washington, D. C.

Dear Sir:

I beg to acknowledge receipt of yours of the second. The publisher of *The Green Book*, my son, is now absent and has temporarily discontinued the publication of *The Green Book* himself although it may be published later on by another party. Agreeable with your request I am sending you the publication of July and August which was the last copy issued.

Kindly acknowledge receipt and oblige,

Yours truly,
Signed   M. M. Levy
for
John V. Levy.

---

85. *The Green Book,* I, No. 1 (May, 1908), 85.
86. *Ibid.*

The cover, size, and type of content of all four issues are very much alike. The first issue contained, in addition to several poems, short stories, and essays, these articles: "Developing Texas" by B. F. Yoakum, "The Galveston Immigration Movement" by Dr. Henry Cohen, and "The Gold Coast," the first of a series of descriptive articles on West Africa by A. Herbert Bowers. There was also a "Publisher's Page," a page of "Mixed Recipes," and a page entitled "Reclamation Service."

Although *The Green Book* might not have been the leading magazine of Texas, as it advertised itself, it was, for the four months that it was published in 1908, among the better ones.

Title: *The Green Book.*
First issue: May, 1908. Last issue: August, 1908.
Periodicity: Monthly.
Editor: John V. Levy.
Publisher: John V. Levy, Galveston.
Size: 25½ cm. Pages: 96.
Price: One dollar per year.

Hunter's Magazine of Frontier History, Border Tragedy, Pioneer Achievement

❧⟨⊚⟩❧

John Warren Hunter was at one time a member of the editorial staff of the *San Angelo Standard*. He was a lover of Texas history, and from the time he was fifteen years old until his death in 1915 he collected Texana—historical sketches from old magazines and newspapers and interviews with old settlers. All this material he kept in large scrapbooks. One day in 1910 he suggested to his son J. Marvin Hunter, who was then publishing a weekly paper in Carlsbad, Texas, that they start a magazine and run frontier stories in it. So *Hunter's Magazine of Frontier History, Border Tragedy, Pioneer Achievement,* printed on a hand press and sewed by hand, was begun with the father, John Warren Hunter, as editor and the son, J. Marvin Hunter, as publisher.[87]

This "Salutatory" appeared on page 12 of Volume I, Number 1, November, 1910:

> Believing that the more than fifty years of Indian Warfare waged by our fathers against savage tribes along the Texas border was a grand panorama of heroic endurance, determination and lofty courage, we bring this magazine before the Texas Public and lay it upon the altar of Texas glory and pioneer renown. We shall write of the sufferings, the hardships and the splendid achievements of pioneer heroes because we are not a stranger to their sorrows, since our feet have trodden many of their stony paths and because we desire, if possible, to hang other garlands upon the brow of those unsung immortals who gathered their laurels from the close and serried ranks of their enemies. To the memory of the Texas pioneer—to the heroic mothers, fathers—to the young and brave who fell fighting manfully for proud, imperial Texas, this humble monument is erected by the unskilled hands of

> The Editor.

---

87. Statements by J. Marvin Hunter, personal interview, Bandera, Texas, August, 1940.

The titles of the articles in the first number were "The Trail of Blood Along and Across the Texas Border"; "Great Indian Raid in Kimble County"; "Murder of J. H. Servell by Indians in 1871"; "Desperate Battle at Nic Coalson's Ranch on Bear Creek"; "Capture and Release of Col. Jack Wilkinson by Comanches"; "With the Sibley Expedition to New Mexico"; and "Thickets Too Small for Indians and White Men."

In April, 1911, the magazine was moved from Carlsbad to Ozona, Texas, where the last issue, Volume II, Number 8, June, 1912, was published.

Financial difficulties made it impossible to continue publishing the magazine. J. Marvin Hunter went to San Antonio to work as a printer. By 1915 he was able to buy another printing plant, at Melvin, Texas. This same year, his father died. But the idea of publishing another historical magazine never left him. He had the large scrapbooks filled with historical material which his father had spent years in collecting. In 1916 J. Marvin Hunter changed the name to *Hunter's Frontier Magazine* and continued or began again the work he and his father had started in 1910. In subject matter and make-up the two magazines were alike. *Hunter's Frontier Magazine* was issued twelve times in 1916—ten times in Melvin and twice in San Antonio.[88] Again Hunter had to admit that a frontier magazine was not a moneymaking proposition. He moved to New Mexico and lived there until 1921. That year he bought a weekly paper in Bandera, Texas, the *Bandera New Era*. In 1922 he bought a linotype and the next year began for the third time a frontier magazine, *Frontier Times*,[89] which is described in a separate section.[90]

> Title: *Hunter's Magazine of Frontier History, Border Tragedy, Pioneer Achievement.*
> First issue: November, 1910. Last issue: June, 1912.
> Title: *Hunter's Frontier Magazine.*
> First Issue: January, 1916. Last issue: December, 1916.
> Periodicity: Monthly.
> Editor: John Warren Hunter, J. Marvin Hunter.
> Publisher: J. Marvin Hunter, Carlsbad, Ozona, Melvin, San Antonio.
> Size: 23 cm. Pages: 20+
> Price: One dollar per year.

---

88. The twelve copies of *Hunter's Frontier Magazine* were examined in Hunter's Museum, Bandera, Texas, August, 1940.

89. Statement by J. Marvin Hunter, personal interview, Bandera, Texas, August, 1940.

90. See page 90.

The Stylus

The Stylus: An Illustrated Weekly Newspaper and Home Magazine: Literary Reviews, Current News, Music, Society, Recreation and the Drama first appeared January 13, 1912. Advertised as the only illustrated weekly magazine in the South, it was published every Saturday by The Stylus Company, Houston; B. H. Carroll, Jr. was editor and Miss Alice Macfarland music editor.

The magazine, varying in size from sixteen to eight large pages, was filled with interesting subject matter; for example, one volume contained among other things an article entitled "War, Wedlock, and Tigers" the subject of which was the war correspondent James F. J. Archibald; a full page poem, "Gold Rust, An Exposition of the Obvious That Mammon Hath Wrought" by Charles Chauncey Carroll, D.D.; on the editorial page, "Autobiography of a Rejected MS." by Everett Lloyd; "The New Mother," a sketch by Theodosia McGraw; "Music and Musings," which included an announcement of a concert that Mme. Luiza Tetrazzini was going to give and a review of a recital given by the boy pianist Pepito Ariola; "News Comments"; "The Drama," with a criticism of "The *Spring Maid* Music" and "The Prince of Tonight"; "Books," a section in which *How To Live On 24 Hours a Day* by Arnold Bennett was reviewed; an essay, "Our Friends of Fiction" by Benjamin Forman; a page bearing the title "Facts and Philosophy"; and several poems scattered throughout.[91]

On the cover of the issue for Saturday, February 24, 1912, another line was added to the title—*Harvey Carroll's Paper*. The magazine was published regularly with little change in the type of material used with this exception: many short stories and several one-act plays eventually found their way into the magazine.

In October, 1912, in "A Heart to Heart Talk with the Readers" the owner and editor discussed "The Old *Stylus* and The New" and announced a change in the form of the magazine:

> The Friends of *The Stylus*, Greeting:
> This issue of *The Stylus* will be the last that will appear in this form of a large, two-color publication. Subsequent

---

91. *The Stylus*, I, No. 3 (January 27, 1912).

issues will be smaller in size and printed in a manner less expensive and on a grade of paper not so costly.

The reason for the change is that to print the paper in its present form and degree of typographical excellence with two color covers involves a cost of approximately $1,000 per month, while the revenues from the paper have run only from $500 to $800 per month. . . .

The Stylus is, and has been for the entire period of its life, the only illustrated literary weekly publication south of Mason and Dixon's line. Its mechanical excellence, composition, lithographs, illustrations in half-tones and all typographical features have been second to no publication printed anywhere, and it is with some genuine regret that the paper abandons for a period the more costly features of its make up. . . .

Most of you have been reading this paper for a number of months.

Is there a place for it?

Is there room for a literary weekly in the South?

Must the entire prosperity of this country be a material prosperity?

Must there be no voice here for things worth while in art and music and poetry and books and life?

Must all one culture be an echo, all of one journalism an adumbration from the North?

The new issue will be two-thirds the present size and will number but eight pages. It will increase in size and in content and in value and in beauty and in worth. You will probably like it. Will you help to make it prosper? If not, then here's wishing you well for past favors.

Sincerely,

B. H. Carroll, Jr.

Owner and Editor.[92]

The smaller *Stylus* without a cover bore this message to the readers:

You tell me there is a place for the paper. It will try to justify your confidence. It will be clean and always an advocate for fair play. It will try to be clever and readable and a vehicle for the best and finest and most wholesome thoughts of the men and women who write in this our Southland. . . .[93]

It is reasonable to assume that even after the size, and therefore the cost, of the magazine was reduced, the editor continued

---

92. *Ibid.*, No. 39 (October 5, 1912), p. 1.
93. *Ibid.*, No. 40 (October 12, 1912), p. 2.

to lose money; for the *New Stylus,* the smaller inexpensive magazine, was issued only eight times, and then *The Stylus* was no more.

Title: *The Stylus: An Illustrated Weekly Newspaper and Home Magazine.*

First issue: January 13, 1912. Last issue: December 7, 1912.

Periodicity: Weekly.

Editor: B. H. Carroll, Jr.

Publisher: The Stylus Co., Houston.

Size: 26, 19 cm. Pages: 16, 8.

Price: One dollar per year.

International Magazine

Another literary magazine that belonged to the San Antonio group was the *International Magazine*. The *International* was primarily a literary magazine, but the editor made an effort "to give somewhere in its pages to each reader something of interest."[94] The first located issue contained poems, stories, and several articles, one of the most readable of which was "The Fiesta San Antonio." In addition to the editorial section, there was one devoted to music and another to drama.[95]

Richard Daughty of Houston wrote so highly of the magazine that the editor, Mrs. Gussie Scott Chaney, quoted him:

> Approximately everything I have ever seen in that magazine is of high quality. For a wonder, even the verse is poetry! I say this without exaggeration. I challenge any one to say it of any other publication of any kind whatsoever in the South. I do not think that the lack of excellent verse in the magazines is wholly due to the fact that none is submitted. I am convinced that it is largely due to the fact that the persons in charge of those publications are as unqualifiedly unfit to recognize excellences in English verse as they would be were it written in Chinese. . . .
>
> I do not know who edits the *International*, but I do know and appreciate the fact that they have restored the traditions, and are touching close upon classicism. . . .[96]

Typical of the type of verse which received praise in the letter above are these two poems:

APRIL[97]

Karl King

She came—and stood upon the threshhold—
A smile about her visage played—
And stern March laughed; his chill breath
    froze her—
And April wept; she was afraid!

---

94. *International Magazine*, VIII, No. 8 (April, 1912), 459.
95. *Ibid.*
96. *Ibid.*, No. 9 (May, 1912), p. 528-529.
97. *Ibid.*, No. 8 (April, 1912), p. 456.

Give Me Love[98]
Louise Adele Carter

Give thy presence to another;
   All the comfort it can prove;
Give them all thy lovely beauty—
   Give me love!

Other gifts from friends and strangers
   Yet however dear they prove,
Only one from thee, beloved
   Give me love!

Love me, though the lands divide us;
   Thee the Southern Cross above;
From the north my lone heart calls thee—
   Give me love!

In April, 1912, according to the May issue, the *International Magazine* bought and paid for the subscription lists and all accounts of the *Bohemian Scribbler*[99] and *State Magazine*.[100] From parts of letters of commendation quoted in this issue, one is led to believe that this magazine had undergone great changes in March, 1912, that the name was changed, and that great improvements were made.[101] The incomplete files of the magazine make it impossible to tell what these changes were, what the name of the magazine was before the change, and what the improvements were. In the *Union List of Serials* all that is said of the magazine is that it continued the *Bohemian Scribbler*.

Title: *International Magazine.*
First issue located: April, 1912. Last issue located: May, 1912.
Periodicity: Monthly.
Editor: Mrs. Gussie Scott Chaney.
Publisher: International Publishing Co., San Antonio.
Size: 17½ cm. Pages: 60.
Price: One dollar per year.

---

98. *Ibid.*, No. 9 (May, 1912), p. 462.
99. See page 67.
100. No copies of the *State Magazine* could be found.
101. *International Magazine*, VIII, No. 9 (May, 1912), 528-529.

The Texas Review—
Southwest Review

The Texas Review, Texas's only early magazine of genuine literary merit, was first published in June, 1915. Robert Adger Law, who edited the magazine for nine years, said of it:

> It was born of a desire on the part of various members of the University of Texas faculty to have some medium of expression for humane endeavor, for Matthew Arnold's "criticism of life." They were convinced that Texas was looked on as a utilitarian state, interested in cotton growing, in stock raising, in oil spudding, but not in spiritual advancement. They believed that this reputation was ill deserved, that Texans have ideals as other men have, but that the outside world knows little of their intellectual strivings. So a group of university professors, with the sympathetic support of their Acting President, determined to found a quarterly review that should set forth these articles of faith.
>
> For editor they chose Stark Young, an energetic young maker and teacher of literature, already author of several slim volumes of poetry.... The managing editor was Percy Houston, another young English teacher and critic, first to dream dreams of the magazine and most enthusiastic and industrious among its founders....[102]

The initial number opened with a long personal letter of congratulation to the editor from Edmund Gosse, the English critic. The editor's salutation was as follows:

> *The Texas Review* comes into the world with no mission, nothing so flamboyant or remonstrant or overt. It has in mind the law of thought and life and letters only; neither to upset nor convert the world, but only to speak with it in its finer and quieter moments. And this review does not dream—it cannot—of great popularity, with subscribers and revolutions, or of pleasing the general, for what begins on nothing but the wish to please the general, ends in being pleased by them.
>
> For the birth of such a venture no small amount of advice was asked, and sometimes taken: to include poetry in a re-

---

102. "The Texas Review, 1915-1924," *Southwest Review*, X, No. 1 (October, 1924), 83-84.

spectable proportion to the other matter; to combine articles of varied interest; to eschew book reviews that are perfunctory and done on a formulary; to open on occasion the doors of our pages without the key of the Phi Beta Kappa. The strongest advice, however, and the most assured, was to let your magazine reek of the soil.

Reeking of the soil is a fine term, no doubt, especially when used by literary experts who never knew the soil. In the sense that the classic myth and classic art and classic poetry are open and clear and inevitable, full of beauty and the tears of things, as is the classic land of myrtles and white rocks and violet sea and hills, the phrase is a good one. In the sense that the old ballad of Chevy Chase is full of heather and frost and border hardihood, well and good. Only, those things seem but the soil flowering into human life. They do not reek. Your reeking is a modern affair, conscious, heavy with journalistic sweat. It is apt to be an exploitation, a marketing.

Say, for example, then, that we should set ourselves to reek of the Texas soil; I have lived in Texas some time and am too near, perhaps, to know how to begin. Like Shylock, these Texans laugh if you tickle them, bleed if you scratch them, and if you wrong them are pretty sure to be revenged. That sort of reeking, then, will include Venice or Israel or England, and will never do. But, then, we have cowboys— in a fraction of the State at least—many of them young fellows with outside beginnings, in some college, some city, some enlightened land or other. I ask them to reek and I get a silly cowboy song, an imitation of Longfellow's worst or of *After the Ball,* cowboy songs whose music or camp setting is well enough, but whose printed form reeks less of the soil than of the semi-poetical worthies of school primers and almanacs.

I find many Texas people hearty and busily rolling their tubs, like Diogenes, in imitation of the national bustle and stir. They remind me of the Golden Age or of Fielding's Squires: they are full of fine scorn sometimes, or of youthful curiosity and concern; they are rarely snobs. I find cultivated people contemplating, or studying softly, or sniffing at life, as is the case elsewhere. The East of Texas is like Mississippi and Ohio and Middle France; the South is like Louisiana and Trieste; Austin is violet and open like Greece; and the West reminds me always of Mexico and North Africa. What then? We shall presently reek of the whole world—ah, that we only could, for that is what true literature has done forever, what we can faintly dream upon as yet.

The one unusual thing in Texas seems to be the opinion at home and abroad that there is something quite unusual about us. There are doubtless *nuances* of experience, varieties of condition, that may appear in our arts, and if the soil of Texas happens to colour finely some literary flower, it will be a fine thing; and yet the Burbank method applied to art, though it may be very chic, is not like Aristippus, mother taught. *The Texas Review* asks of the critic and of some provincial citizens of the world, patience if we do not always reek.

The Editor.[103]

The contents of the June number were, besides Edmund Gosse's letter and the editor's salutation, "The End of Summer," a formerly unpublished poem by Madison Cawein; "In the Trenches," a poem by Maurice Hewlett; "Poet's Song," a poem by Charlotte Wilson; "Poems" by Eunice Tietjens; "An Illustration of Madison Cawein's Poetry" by James Finch Royster; "The Case Against Great Britain—in the Light of Her History" by Thad W. Riker; "In Your Letters" by Tucker Brooke; "The Pump Room"; "A Paper on Pedants" by Carl Van Doren; and "The Negro Chain Gang" by Margaret Law.

Page 2 of the first issue had this to say about contributors:

Tucker Brooke, Assistant Professor of English at Yale University. Author of *The Shakespeare Apochrypha* and of *The Tudor Drama*.

Carl Van Doren, Assistant Professor in English, Columbia University. Author of *A Life of Thomas Love Peacock*.

Lindley Miller Keasbey, Professor of Institutional History in the University of Texas. Author of *The Nicaragua Canal and the Monroe Doctrine* and other works.

Edmund Gosse, English critic and poet and essayist. Author of *Jacobean Studies, A History of Eighteenth Century Literature, Father and Son*.

Madison Cawein, the late Kentucky poet. Author of many books of verse.

Maurice Hewlett, English poet and novelist. Author of *Richard Yea and Nay, The Queen's Quair, Helen Redeemed* and other works.

Charlotte Wilson, of Nacogdoches, Texas, frequent contributor of verse and prose to American magazines, winner of several literary prizes.

Eunice Tietjens, frequent contributor of verse to periodicals, assistant editor of *Poetry*.

---

103. "On Reeking of the Soil," *The Texas Review*, I, No. 1 (June, 1915), 80-81.

James Finch Royster, Professor of English at the University of Texas.

Thad W. Riker, Adjunct Professor of Modern European History at the University of Texas. Author of *A Life of Henry Fox, First Lord Holland.*

Margaret Law, of Philadelphia, is a recent graduate of Wellesley.

To quote again from Dr. Law's history of *The Texas Review:*

In its first issue, then, *The Texas Review* established the policy of printing considerable verse as well as prose, and practically all its prose was written by college professors. It carried informal essays together with serious criticism, and it studiously avoided the formal book review.

The second number, the last one edited by Young, is distinctly less Texan in its flavor, containing notable contributions from Sir Gilbert Murray, Josephine Preston Peabody, Max Eastman, Richard Burton, Alvin S. Johnson, and H. C. Chatfield-Taylor. Practically all these men and women were personal friends of Mr. Young outside of Texas, and he naturally desired to print the matter that they had furnished him before his retirement from the editorial chair. But the collection of their writings in a single number raised two difficulties for those who inherited the *Review:* it set a standard of literary excellence which the *Review* has never since been able to reach in one issue, and it left the cupboard almost bare of the finest material for publication that had been nearly a year in gathering. . . .

When in September, 1915, the editorial board of the *Review* met to plan for its future, they faced the task of filling the places of both editor and manager, for Mr. Young and Mr. Houston, each, left the University of Texas during the summer to accept teaching positions in Eastern colleges.[104]

To carry on the *Review* under these circumstances was regarded by the Board as a patriotic duty. Subscribers had generally paid one year ahead, and contributors had offered their wares *gratis* after much personal solicitation. . . .

In choosing Young's successor the Board considered enlisting two men for joint service. . . .on a certain memorably warm afternoon in early October, 1915, [they] drafted me for the job. . . .

The rest of the story is known fairly well to our Constant

---

104. Stark Young resigned his position in Texas to become Professor of English in Amherst College, Massachusetts. The managing editor, Percy H. Houston, assumed the professorship of English in Acadia University, Nova Scotia.

Readers. If the *Review* had any excuse for being, it must foster thought and criticism in Texas and the Southwest. While it would not close the doors of hope on writers from any quarter, it was founded to provide hospitality to Texans who could express thoughts of cultural interest to other Texans, without, to use Mr. Young's phrase, "reeking of the soil.". . .

To further the cause of genuine culture by making easier the publication of such material in Texas, and to advertise to outsiders our interest in these subjects have been guiding principles in the *Review*'s editorial conduct. Unfortunately, abundance of suitable "copy" was not always on hand. As years went on and its original promoters moved away, the group of those willing to contribute articles and solicit contributions from their literary acquaintance grew smaller and less energetic. Notable exceptions to this last statement have been Benjamin Mather Woodbridge and Howard Mumford Jones, whose activity in providing or securing matter of publication seemed never to.flag. . . .

The prospect of better days for *The Texas Review* at its new home in Dallas has substantial basis. [The *Review* was transferred to Southern Methodist University in August, 1924, Volume X, Number 1.] Editor Hubbell and Associate Editor Bond, already contributors, are excellently qualified by zeal and knowledge to foster throughout Texas and the Southwest the creation of literature and criticism. Moreover, the list of advisory editors [105] already made public assures them the backing of a definitive group possessing faith in the cause and willing to show their faith by their works. Particularly, the story of active service of Southern Methodist University and the city of Dallas in stimulating the production of poetry heartens every friend of humane culture in the state. Such a situation calls for a larger medium of expression. Those who have long labored earnestly, however ineffectively, to maintain the *Review* may soon realize their larger hopes.[106]

When *The Texas Review* was moved from The University of Texas to Southern Methodist University, its name was changed to *Southwest Review*. The new editor, Jay B. Hubbell, in his salutation "The New Southwest," dedicated the pages of the new *Texas Review* to the younger Southwest and said:

---

105. Karle Wilson Baker, John O. Beaty, Pierce Butler, Witter Bynner, Robert Adger Law, John H. McGinnis, J. W. Rogers, Frederick D. Smith, J. Frank Dobie, Hilton Ross Greer, Easley S. Jones, John Clark Jordan.

106. "The Texas Review," *Southwest Review*, X, No. 1 (October, 1924), 85-90.

In spite of many difficulties, which outsiders can hardly appreciate, Mr. Young, Dr. Law, and their associates have set a worthy standard which the incoming editors will do their best to uphold. Inevitably, however, when any magazine passes into the hands of a new board of editors, there will be certain changes in its character. May we submit to our readers our somewhat random reflections and invite their criticism of the policy indicated below? In formulating a policy, we have given much thought to the relation which a Southwestern magazine should bear to the section which it endeavors to represent. To us at least it seems clear that the success of the *Southwest Review* depends largely upon its adaptation to the *milieu* from which it springs.[107]

The *Southwest Review*, then, will be national in its outlook, and its pages will be open to all who write well; but it will especially encourage those who write on Western themes, for it is a magazine for the Southwest. We shall strive, most of all, for variety and, without being journalistic, for timeliness. The editor will welcome readable articles dealing with literature, art, politics, social affairs, religion, education, and business. The *Review* will occasionally print short stories or short plays, and it will run all the good verse that it can get. It will now and then print articles that make a substantial contribution to scholarship even at the risk of occasionally boring a desultory reader; but it will not be a repository for professional articles that no one wants to read. It is on the basis of such a policy as we have indicated that we appeal for the support of contributors and readers.[108]

True to the aim stated in Jay B. Hubbell's salutation, the *Southwest Review* has since striven for variety and timeliness and has emphasized Texas and the Southwest. But even with emphasis placed on the Southwest, the *Southwest Review* did not limit itself in scope.

In keeping with its wide aim the "Special Poetry Number"[109] contained poems by John Gould Fletcher, Harriet Monroe, Edwin Ford Piper, George Sterling, Lizette Woodworth Reese, John Crowe Ransom, Grace Noll Crowell, Lucia Trent, Jake Zeitlin, Constance Lindsey Skinner, William Russell Clark, Karle Wilson Baker, John Drinkwater, Gamaliel Bradford, Lew Sarett, Peggy Pond, and Stanley Vestal.

In Volume XII, Number 3, April, 1927, John H. McGinnis's

107. *Ibid.*, p. 91.
108. *Ibid.*, pp. 98-99.
109. *Ibid.*, X, No. 3 (April, 1925).

name was included with Jay B. Hubbell's as editor. In Volume XIII, Number 1, October, 1927, the editors listed were John H. McGinnis, Henry Smith, and John Chapman. By January, 1933, the editors numbered five: John H. McGinnis, Henry Smith, Charles W. Pipkin, William A. Read, and S. D. Myres, Jr. In this January issue, which was Volume XVIII, Number 2, the announcement was made that the quarterly was published by Southern Methodist University and Louisiana State University; however, Louisiana State University was not named as a publisher in Volume XXI, Number 1, Autumn, 1935. By October, 1936, Volume XXI, Number 4, the number of editors had increased to seven: John H. McGinnis, Henry Smith, S. D. Myres, Jr., George Bond, John W. Bowyer, J. Frank Dobie, Stanley Vestal. In Volume XXII, Number 4, July, 1937, Ernest E. Leisy's name was added to the list of editors.

An editorial in Volume XXX, Number 1, Autumn, 1944, referred to Jay B. Hubbell's goal for the magazine as stated in Volume X, Number 1, October, 1924, and concluded as follows:

> For twenty years the *Review* has followed this program brilliantly and effectively.... The present editor feels that the *Review* like a University is going to have to gear itself more closely to life. This will not demand a radical change in the original program announced by Professor Hubbell; rather it will be an expanding of that program to meet the needs of a developing region and a changing world.

In Volume L, Number 2, Spring, 1965, Margaret L. Hartley, the first woman editor, wrote in "The Editor's Notebook":

> ...I believe the SWR should be "regional"—expressing our awareness of our region and of the nation and the world, in writing originating in our area and also in a choice of writing from elsewhere that conveys, by the very nature of its selections, the way we see things from "our plot of earth" as Dobie called it....
>
> We shall attempt, then, to be alert always to all that makes up the present—and this includes the past. SWR will continue to be profoundly engaged with what is going on not only in literature, but in social and economic and every other sort of life in the present....

In keeping with the objectives of *The Texas Review*, later the *Southwest Review*, as expressed by the editors, the magazine has emphasized the regional, and at the same time national, point of view. Through the years, the articles of sectional interest, the poems, essays, stories, plays, criticisms, book reviews, articles on art and artists, and sketches of contributors who are often nationally and internationally known have made this publication the outstanding magazine contribution of Texas to the literary world.

Title: *The Texas Review, Southwest Review.*
First issue: June, 1915. Last issue: Current.
Periodicity: Quarterly.
Editors: Stark Young, Robert Adger Law, George Bond, Jay B. Hubbell, and others.
Publishers: The University of Texas, Austin. Southern Methodist University, Dallas.
Size: 16 cm.+ Pages: 100+.
Price: Two dollars per year. Three dollars per year.

Grinstead's Graphic

Born in Kentucky in 1856, J. E. Grinstead moved to the Hill Country of Texas in 1899. When he was fifty years old, he wrote his first novel. Sixteen other novels with a distinctive Texas flavor followed. Most of these stories were published first as serials in such magazines as the *Argosy, Everybody's Magazine, All Western,* and *Western Romance* and later in book form.[110]

This man, J. E. Grinstead, editor and publisher of *Grinstead's Graphic,* once declared that he did not believe much in what some highbrowed people have been pleased to call the "Urge" to do things.[111] He said the finest urge he ever had was need of whiskey and tobacco; these two needs were his only inspiration. He added that he did not like to write, that in fact there was nothing he liked to do, and that if he could afford to, he would just sit and not even draw breath.[112]

He did admit, however, that his magazine, the *Graphic,* was the child of that inexplicable driving power, the "Urge."

> In January, 1921, when the whole world looked like a dreary, darksome plain, and mighty, forbidding hills loomed on every hand; when men were appalled by the apparent magnitude of their losses, the "Urge" came to me. There seemed a very real voice, saying: "God made you a jester, and it is but fair that you lighten the burdens of His people when they are in tribulation."[113]

So in a time of financial depression, the time when magazines generally die, *Grinstead's Graphic* was born.

This salutation was given under the title "Rules of the Game":

> Get this. *Grinstead's Graphic* is just what its name implies. Every syllable in it is written by the editor. Contributions are not wanted, and will not be accepted under any circumstances. This applies also to poetry, which is admittedly the lowest order of human expression except making

---

110. Statement by J. E. Grinstead, personal interview, Kerrville, August, 1940.

111. *Grinstead's Graphic,* II, No. 1 (January, 1922), 5.

112. Statement by J. E. Grinstead, personal interview, Kerrville, August, 1940.

113. *Grinstead's Graphic,* II, No. 1 (January, 1922), 5.

signs or shaking a bush. The editor of the *Graphic* has two serious bilious spells each year; one in the spring and one in the fall, about the time goats are sheared. At such periods some poetry may be expected. Otherwise, these pages will be devoted to fiction, fact, and frankly expressed opinion.

The editorial policy of the *Graphic* will be the same as that adhered to by its editor throughout a long career in the newspaper field. No man living can dictate or influence one word of it.

The purpose of this publication is to help, and not to hinder. To cause smiles when possible, and if any tears, only such as wash the cobwebs from the windows of the heart, and let God's sunshine in.[114]

The first number, issued in January, 1921, contained besides the salutation an article called "The Tariff"; the first installment of a serial, "Two Bits"; and three philosophical articles: "The Inside of a Dollar," "Taking Our Losses," and "A Smile or Two."

When the magazine had been in existence for six months, the editor wrote:

Speaking of going things, when I started the *Graphic* some of my friends told me I had a lot of nerve to start a new enterprise in such a crisis. They were mistaken. I am a timid old scout. I just had a lot of confidence in my people. I knew them better than they knew themselves. . . . The *Graphic* is going good. There are about three thousand people reading it now, including those who borrow it from their neighbors. Let them borrow it! If it didn't do them good they wouldn't want to read it. Doing good is the main thing it is published for. . . .[115]

At the end of the third year he wrote:

The *Graphic* is now three years old. With the January number it will be a three-year-old, coming four. It has all its grass teeth cut, and the range is good, so why should anybody worry. There are but few who read the first number that are not still reading it. The *Graphic* is a magazine of the Hill Country. The people of the Hill Country are its audience, and its chief supporters. It is the purpose of the *Graphic* to please the people of this section of Texas in particular, and as many others as it can.[116]

The people of Texas must have found the Western serials entertaining, shared the enthusiasm of the editor for the Hill Country, wanted to be told the beauty and value of smiling and the

---

114. *Ibid.*, I, No. 1 (January, 1921), 3.
115. *Ibid.*, No. 6 (June, 1921), 6-7.
116. *Ibid.*, III, No. 12 (December, 1925), 3.

futility of worry, and found the occasional poems interesting. Perhaps it was encouraging to know that in the face of a depression one man at least could still write such sentences as these: "Looking at it from here, it ain't so bad,"[117] "When you leave 1921, trade your grouch for a smile—and use it,"[118] and "There is nothing more beautiful than Sunlight on Green Hills—and smiles."[119]

In May, 1924,[120] the size of the magazine was enlarged. The blue-green cover was changed to a light yellow one. On the cover was a square with a heart inside it. Inscribed on the heart were these words: "Heart o' the Hills Magazine Published Monthly at Kerrville, Texas."

The "Au Revoir, But Not Good-bye" was said in these words in the December, 1925, issue:

> Well, fellows, this is the last time you will read *Grinstead's Graphic*, for a while at least. I'm not sore about anything. *Graphic* has been doing all right, but. . . . Fact of the matter is I have been publishing something or other for more than thirty years. I won't say how much more . . . in those long years I got woefully behind with my resting. I want to rest awhile. I thought when I changed from a weekly[121] to a monthly publication that I might catch up that way, but it seems not. I'm still tired. Maybe I'll get out an annual number of the *Graphic* for a few years, just to let you know that I'm not a quitter. . . .

And Grinstead meant it when he said it was "Au Revoir, But Not Good-bye," for the *Graphic* was not first published in 1921 but in 1912; and the last issue was not in 1925 but in 1940. From 1921 to 1925 the *Graphic* was published monthly and the volumes and numbers were given. But as Grinstead has said: "It had no beginning, no end."[122] Occasional numbers were published before and after the time of the regularly numbered *Graphic*. These publications, not numbered, were advertising, moneymaking propositions.

---

117. *Ibid.*, I, No. 8 (August, 1921), cover.

118. *Ibid.*, I, No. 12 (December, 1921), cover.

119. *Ibid.*, III, No. 8 (August, 1923), cover.

120. *Ibid.*, IV, No. 5 (May, 1924).

121. *Grinstead's Graphic* from I, 1, January, 1921, through V, 12, December, 1925, was a monthly publication. Grinstead here refers to prior publication.

122. Statement by J. E. Grinstead, personal interview, Kerrville, August, 1940.

Title: *Grinstead's Graphic.*

First issue: January, 1921. Last issue (regular series): December, 1925.

Periodicity: Monthly.

Editor: J. E. Grinstead.

Publisher: J. E. Grinstead, Kerrville.

Size: 15½ cm. Pages: 40.

Price: One dollar and a half per year.

Frontier Times

J. Marvin Hunter, who had published *Hunter's Magazine* from 1910 to 1912 and had edited and published *Hunter's Frontier Magazine* in 1916, began editing and publishing *Frontier Times* in October, 1923. The magazine, like its two predecessors, was "Devoted to Frontier History, Border Tragedy and Pioneer Achievement." The *Frontier Times* was printed on newsprint and bound in very thin light tan or yellow paper. The cover carried—in addition to the date, volume, number, price, title and subtitle, and publisher—a picture of some person important in frontier history.

The purpose of the magazine as given by the publisher was as follows:

> You have before you the first number of *Frontier Times,* a monthly magazine devoted to Frontier History, Border Tragedy and Pioneer Achievement. It shall be the object of this magazine from month to month, and from year to year, to place on record a continuous account of the daring deeds of the heroes of Texas, and in this we make no claims to originality of matter. We have gleaned from all authentic sources within our reach, interesting and important incidents which have transpired since the first appearance of the European in Texas to the conclusion of Indian wars on our frontiers in which our countrymen have borne a part. We shall endeavor to give these incidents in detail and in pleasing form, our aim being to produce a magazine of instruction, attractive and popular reading—to embalm in the memory of Texan youth the sacrifices, the patriotism, the heroism, the suffering and dangers of those to whom we owe the achievement and preservation of our freedom. . . . It is our object to perpetuate this sentiment [a spirit of reverence and gratitude to heroic fathers for liberty] to keep burning bright the fires upon the altar of patriotism; succeeding in this our ends will have been accomplished.[123]

Proof that Mr. Hunter was sure of having enough material to keep his magazine going for years was given in these words of his:

---

123. *Frontier Times,* I, No. 1 (October, 1923), 32.

Some of our friends have expressed the opinion that the material which goes to make *Frontier Times* so popular and the only publication of its kind in the world, will, in the course of a few months, be totally exhausted. We would admonish them to have no uneasiness on this score. Already we have in manuscript, material enough to run for several years, and by a systematic plan new stories are being constantly received and filed for future use. Your grandchildren will read *Frontier Times* with the same degree of interest you manifested when you read your last number while your worthy neighbor across the way was waiting to borrow it so that he and his neighbor might learn of the daring deeds by those forefathers and mothers who wrested this fair land from the painted savage and bequeathed it to this generation. We have with us yet many of these brave pioneers, who, though bent with the weight of years, have not forgotten the hardships endured and the dangers courted to extend the bounds of civilization, and of them we would voice praises and freely use the columns of our Magazine to perpetuate the glory of their achievement....[124]

When the *Frontier Times* was in its second year, J. Frank Dobie, writing of the magazine, made this comment:

Whatever loss to the record of dialect the changing of fashion of fiction may have entailed, is, however, more than compensated for by the increasing number of chronicles and biographies from the folk themselves. Hundreds of words, metaphors, sayings common to the pioneer stock of the Southwest can be gleaned from such a homely and interesting magazine as *Frontier Times,* edited and published by Mr. J. Marvin Hunter of Bandera, Texas.[125]

The contents of Volume I, Number 1, were "Jack Hays, the Famous Texas Ranger"; "The Trail of Blood Along the Texas Border"; "The Massacre of John Webster and Party"; "History of Fort Inge, on the Leona River"; "Taming the Savage Apache Followers of Geronimo"; "A Dunce of the Eighties—the Diamond King"; "Population of Texas Seventy-five Years Ago"; "Arizona Indian Wars"; "The Cry of the Death Bird Served as a Warning"; "The Lipan Indian Tribe"; "Old Dances in Vogue"; "The Hunt for the Bowie Mine in Menard"; "Remarkable Life Story of Quanah Parker"; and "Belief in the Efficacy of the Madstone." These articles were by different contributors; some were clippings from newspapers, others were written by the editor.

---

124. *Ibid.,* No. 3 (January, 1924), p. 48.
125. *Frontier Times,* II, No. 6 (March, 1925), 32.

The frontiersman, Indian raids, Texas Rangers and their work, heroines of early Texas, and the Texas pioneer continued to be the popular subjects for the articles. In August, 1940, Mr. Hunter reported that in the seventeen volumes of the *Frontier Times*, "The Chronicler of Neglected History," over 5,000 historical sketches had appeared.[126]

In May, 1946, Volume XXIII, Number 8, J. Marvin Hunter, Sr., was listed as editor and J. Marvin Hunter, Jr., as publisher. The announcement was made that the new headquarters for the magazine was Baird, Texas. A full page advertisement from the Baird Chamber of Commerce bade the magazine welcome.

In Volume XXX, Number 1, January, 1953, on pages 1 and 2, there was a special greeting as follows:

> *Frontier Times* greets you in its new dress and format, and from its new publication headquarters in Grand Prairie. For twenty-nine years this magazine has been published as a monthly, but has now been changed to a quarterly, and will come to you in January, April, July, October of each year. . . .
>
> *Frontier Times* has always been printed in a country printing office, where our facilities were very limited. First, it was published at Bandera, Texas, for more than twenty years . . . then for eight years it was published in the office of the *Baird Star*. . . . In the twenty-nine years we have been publishing *Frontier Times* we have printed more than 15,000 pages of authentic Texas history, which has met the approval of historians everywhere. . . .

The greeting pointed out the fact that *Frontier Times* was a family affair: J. Marvin Hunter, Sr., was the managing editor; J. Marvin Hunter, Jr., was the publisher and business manager; Jack M. Hunter was the assistant business manager and shop foreman; and Mrs. J. Marvin Hunter, Jr., was the bookkeeper and circulation manager. However, J. Marvin Hunter, Sr., founder and editor, was to continue to reside in Bandera, Texas, where he was owner of Frontier Times Museum, and all articles intended for publication in the *Frontier Times* were to be addressed to him there.

Volume XXXI, Number 4, October, November, and December, 1954, was the last number published by the Frontier Times Publishing House in Grand Prairie with J. Marvin Hunter, Sr., editor and J. Marvin Hunter, Jr., publisher. With this issue the "Hunter family affair" came to an end.

---

126. Statement by J. Marvin Hunter, personal interview, Bandera, Texas, August, 1940.

J. Marvin Hunter, Sr., died in 1957. That same year there appeared a larger magazine *Frontier Times,* Winter, 1957-1958, Volume XXXII, Number 1, New Series Number 1. According to this issue the magazine was published quarterly by Western Publications, Austin, Texas; the publisher was Joe Austell Small, and the editor was Norman B. Wiltsey.

A letter from the editor on the first page under the title "Here It Is At Last" was in part as follows:

> What with magazines falling out all around us—some of them the very biggest—it makes our "scared box" bubble over with goose pimples to come out with a new magazine right now.
>
> But with thousands of you yelling for *True West* magazine to be published monthly we had to do something....
>
> ...We decided to keep *True West* like it was and revive a magazine that was started by the late Marvin Hunter in 1923, making it quarterly to begin with and gradually ease it into bi-monthly.... Actually *Frontier Times* and *True West* will be practically the same magazine—*True West* will come out one month—*Frontier Times* the next.

Although the magazine still carries the title *Frontier Times,* it was, after it was revived, much more a true west magazine than it was the frontier magazine J. Marvin Hunter, Sr., had created and published.

> Title: *Frontier Times.*
> First issue: October, 1923. Last issue: Current.
> Periodicity: Monthly, quarterly.
> Editors: J. Marvin Hunter, Sr., Norman B. Wiltsey, Joe Austell Small, Pat Wagner.
> Publishers: J. Marvin Hunter, Sr., Bandera; J. Marvin Hunter, Jr., Baird; Norman B. Wiltsey, Grand Prairie; Joe Austell Small, Austin.
> Size: 21 cm., 26 cm. Pages: 32-72.
> Price: One dollar and fifty cents per year, two dollars per year, three dollars per year.

The Woman's Viewpoint

The Woman's Viewpoint: A Magazine Serving Humanity, Edited and Published by Women was dedicated to:

> ... the love of justice, love of right, love of mercy, and pity for the suffering, to assist the weak, to forget wrongs and remember benefits, to love the truth, to love sincerity, to love honest words, to love liberty, to wage relentless war against war in all its forms; to the love of Mother, of Father and of Child and of Friend. To make happy homes, to create the love of the beautiful in nature, in art, to help cultivate the mind to be familiar with the mighty thoughts that genius has expressed, to cultivate courage and cheerfulness, to make others happy, to fill lives with the splendor of generous acts; to destroy the error of prejudice, to receive new truths with gladness and to cultivate hope. To see the silver lining beyond the clouds and storm, to do the best we can at all times, and to trust God for the result.[127]

Its purpose was

> To Be international in scope, uncompromising in principle and liberal enough to voice the varying constructive thoughts of women all over the world.
> To Give a constructive survey of the whole field of women's interest.
> To Help bring about a better understanding between women of all nations.
> To Be non-partisan in politics.
> To Express the viewpoint of women everywhere.[128]

Florence M. Sterling founded her magazine in 1923 in Houston. The magazine was designed to please women. Its more-or-less regular features were "Cat Claws," "Counselor," "Your Baby's Welfare," "Who's Who in Schools," "Women Everywhere," "Hostess Helps," "Fashion Fancies," "In the World of Books," "Music Notes," "Health and Beauty," "Little Citizens Club," "Shopper's Guide," and "Movie Mention." The special features were political discussions by the editor, a series of articles entitled "America's Twelve Greatest Women," biographical sketches of outstanding Texans, and poetry (including the work of Grace Noll

---

127. *The Woman's Viewpoint*, I, No. 11 (March 12, 1924), 4.
128. *Ibid.*, IV, No. 3 (July, 1926), 5.

Crowell, the Texas poet, and Will Allen Dromgoole of Tennessee). The many illustrations and the cover design in color added much to the appearance of the magazine.

Perhaps the fact that the magazine was published first weekly, then semi-monthly, and finally monthly helps to explain how it grew from a magazine of 22 to 90 pages. In March, 1926, Florence Sterling moved her magazine to Albany, New York, where she continued publishing it until September of that year.

Title: *The Woman's Viewpoint.*

First issue located: March 12, 1924. Last issue: September, 1926.

Periodicity: Weekly. Semi-monthly. Monthly.

Editor: Florence M. Sterling.

Publisher: Florence M. Sterling, The Woman's Viewpoint Publishing Co., Inc., Houston, Texas (March, 1924–February, 1926); Albany, New York (March, 1926–September, 1926).

Size: 23½ cm. Pages: 20-90.

Price: One dollar per year. Three dollars per year.

The Buccaneer

One of the outstanding poetry journals published in Texas was *The Buccaneer,* which William Russell Clark began in Dallas in September, 1924. This journal paid for no poems, paid no editorial salaries, served no cliques, and lived only to nourish the best poetic growth of the Southwest and to serve as a forum of American poets.[129] It did not live in vain, for a study of its contributors reveals such Texas poets as Lexie Dean Robertson, Jan Isbelle Fortune, Grace Noll Crowell, Hilton Ross Greer, as well as Aubrey Burns, Ruth Maxwell, and Dawson Powell—members of the "Makers," the poetry group of Southern Methodist University in Dallas. Among the well-known poets out of the state who contributed to the journal were Mary Carolyn Davies, John Gould Fletcher, John Drinkwater, William Rose Benét, Marguerite Wilkinson, Hervey Allen, Lizette Woodworth Reese, and Joseph Auslander.

The editor was interested

> ... primarily in finding writers of ordinary intelligence and ability who are new enough not to be foolish, and old enough not to be freakish. And when we find writers meeting these specifications, we lasso them into the family circle and welcome them into the cabin of *The Buccaneer* to meet a large and growing crew where intellect is not measured by youth or old age, but by adequate and reputable poetic expression and interpretation.[130]

The announcement was made in the June-July publication[131] that *The Buccaneer* would suspend activities until fall, when publication would be resumed as usual. But Volume II, Number 1, did not appear until the first part of the year 1926. When it did appear, Dawson Powell was editor and the following announcement was made:

> With this issue, Volume II, Number 1, *The Buccaneer* begins its career as a quarterly. Since publication was suspended under the editorship of William Russell Clark with Volume I, Number 10-11, the affairs of the magazine have

---

129. *The Buccaneer,* II, No. 3-4 (July-December, 1926), 27.
130. *Ibid.,* I, No. 2 (October, 1924), 28.
131. *Ibid.,* No. 10 (June-July, 1925), p. 31.

undergone a reorganization. The change came about without mutiny. Mr. Clark had directed the policy of the magazine and borne the financial burden of publishing it until the cost of the venture became too great for one person to carry alone. When Mr. Clark suspended publication he requested his associates to do all possible to carry on. We are happy to announce that it has been possible to put the magazine on a sound business basis and that while the supply of worthwhile poetry continues and our subscribers bear with us we shall expect to publish regularly, four times each year.[132]

Further announcements were made that changes in the general policies of the magazine were to be negligible; subscriptions were to be carried over; those who were due six monthly issues were to receive six quarterly issues; and the new editors were not assuming the responsibility of annual prizes which had been announced.

Volume II, Number 2, was dated April, May, June, 1926; Volume II, Numbers 3 and 4, were dated July-December, 1926. By this time the journal was in financial difficulties. The twelve guarantors had dwindled to three. The editor's plan was to obtain ten supporting-subscribers who were to pay $100 each and twenty supporting-subscribers who would pay $50 each in order for the magazine to have an uninterrupted period of growth.[133] His plan was evidently a failure, for *The Buccaneer* ceased publication.

Besides the poety in *The Buccaneer* there was a book review section in which the outstanding poetry publications were reviewed, an editorial section, and a section entitled "Notes on Contributors."

Title: *The Buccaneer: A Journal of Poetry.*
First issue: September, 1924. Last issue: July-December, 1926.
Periodicity: Monthly. Quarterly.
Editors: William Russell Clark, Dawson Powell.
Publishers: William Russell Clark and Dawson Powell, Dallas.
Size: 16½ cm. Pages: 32-40.
Price: Four dollars per year. One dollar per year.

---

132. *Ibid.*, II, No. 1 (January, February, March, 1926), 26.
133. *Ibid.*, No. 3-4 (July-December, 1926), p. 27.

The Texas Argus

It is difficult to tell just what Clyde Wantland had in mind when he was editing *The Texas Argus*. Did he intend for this magazine to be a general, a political, a reform, or a literary magazine?

The table of contents as given on the cover for the March, 1928, issue is as follows:

> When the Indian Got Religion
>> Franciscan Fathers found Texas Redskin at heart merely a plain Methodist: Lost one day and saved the next. Effort to salvage him abandoned after 100 years tussle.
>
> "Turn-the-Rascals-Out" Jim Reed
>> Inveterate foe of frauds, hypocrites, crooks, and Republicans just now has politicians pondering what to do with him at Houston.
>
> Proper Way to Kill a Community Chest
>> Social workers draw lessons from fatal illness of San Antonio's recently deceased agency.
>
> Some Laws That the Governor Breaks
>> Ex-candidate says most offcials would be in penitentiary if Texas election laws were enforced even partially.
>
> A Short-Story by O. Henry
>> The Princess and the Puma
>
> Book Reviews
>> Will Durant's "Transition" - "American Journalism" - "Gutzon Borglum and Stone Mountain."

Another story by O. Henry, "The Reformation of Calliope," appeared in the other issue examined.[134] Even though the O. Henry stories were reprints, they gave the magazine some claim at least to the term literary.

> Title: *The Texas Argus*.
> First issue: March, 1928. Last issue: April, 1928.
> Periodicity: Monthly.
> Editor: Clyde Wantland.
> Publisher: Argus Publishing Co. Inc., San Antonio.
> Size: 17 cm. Pages: 30.
> Price: Twenty-five cents per copy. Fifteen cents per copy.

---

134. *The Texas Argus*, II, No. 3 (April, 1928), 4-18.

The Aclavache
⚜

In the fall of 1928 Charlie Jeffries moved to Austin in order to be a part of Texas's great center of learning. His ambition was to establish a magazine to be called *The Aclavache,* a word coined by the editor. The yearly subscription was to be two dollars, one dollar of which was collected in advance. After one issue Jeffries returned the dollar to the three people who had subscribed in advance and explained that no more issues would be published, as there was no financial support.[135]

On the editorial page of the magazine, the editor in a discussion of the publication's purpose and expectation said:

> The first and most vital cause for duration is the financial one, for the single reason that no business of this kind can last long that is not self sustaining. Another incentive to venture is the plain, unaffected pleasure of making a magazine, getting out a worthwhile, readable sheet.
>
> A broader, and what to the public may be a more interesting reason, is to try to develop here in Texas, a literature of a distinct, native type. This is the ulterior motive.
>
> That there is plenty of talent here, hardly needs to be stated; but this talent, in instances where it is cultivated and employed, nearly always shows effects of outside training. This is not meant as finding fault with the literary style of other sections; but the genius of Texas is not the genius of the North and East. A thousand miles difference in ancestry can not but work a difference in ways of thinking; and best results can never be had by copying the method of other folk. If we are to produce any thing really great, we must cut loose from restraints that do not fit us, and strike out for ourselves; looking on the world boldly with our own eyes; and, without turning to right or left for approbation, express ourselves in our own way.
>
> This is not an invitation to crudeness of thought or license to looseness of grammar, nor is it any disparagement to the fundamental principles of the great writing art; but in ideas and tastes, it is an appeal to the unfettered originality of the Southwest.[136]

---

135. Statement by J. Frank Dobie, personal interview, Austin, Texas, April, 1940.

136. *The Aclavache,* I, No. 1 (March, 1929).

This issue contained thirty pages bound in white thin paper; only the title and the date were printed on the cover. The contents were as follows: "Road Evolution in Texas," an essay by Charlie Jeffries; "Won't You Tell Me a Story?" a story by Laura Davis Mobley; "The Small Streams of East Texas," a poem by Bessie K. Osborn; "Some Noted Rangers," an historical essay by Dick Ware; "Editorial Page"; "The Stone of Tehuacana Hills," a poem by Whitney Montgomery; "The Fatalist," a poem by John Pirie; "Confetti" and "Coral Sands," poems by Juliet Jayne; "Retreat From Meekness," a poem by David Cornell De Jong; "Birth Stars," a short story by Charlie Jeffries; "The Jester," a poem by Frances A. Keith; "The Greek Men," a story by London Glick; and "Looking Ahead," a short essay, with no author given.

The magazine was published in Austin in March, 1929.

> Title: *The Aclavache.*
> First issue: March, 1929. Last issue: March, 1929.
> Periodicity: Monthly.
> Editor: Charlie Jeffries.
> Publisher: Charlie Jeffries, Austin.
> Size: 20 cm. Pages: 30.
> Price: Two dollars per year.

Appendix

The following list includes all the magazines discussed in the preceding pages, with the dates of beginning and ending, if known, or the dates of the earliest and latest issues located. The names of the libraries in which files of the magazines are to be found are given for only those magazines *not* listed in the *Union List of Serials* (those so listed are designated "ULS"). Only the first place of publication is given.

MAGAZINE	DATE EARLIEST ISSUE	FIRST PLACE PUBLISHED	DATE LAST ISSUE	LIBRARY CONTAINING FILES
Texian Monthly Magazine	July, 1858	Galveston	September, 1858	ULS
Allan's Texas Monthly	June, 1867	Houston	June, 1867	ULS
The Stylus	February, 1876	Austin	June, 1876	ULS
The American Sketch Book	No month given, 1878	Austin	1883	ULS
The Amaranth	March, 1882	Dallas	March, 1882	ULS
The Prairie Flower	July, 1882	Corsicana	June, 1885	ULS
The Guardian and Young Texan	October, 1884	Waco	October, 1884	Texas Collection, University of Texas; Baylor University
The Lone Star Magazine	March, 1887	Dallas	April, 1887	ULS
The Repository	August, September, October, 1889	Austin	August, September, October, 1889	Texas Collection, University of Texas
The Round Table	April, 1890	Dallas	March, 1893	Texas Collection, University of Texas
The Guardian	January, 1891	Waco	December, 1895	Texas Collection, University of Texas
The Gulf Messenger	January, 1892	San Antonio	February, March, 1898	ULS
The Period—Lee's Texas Magazine	August, 1893	Dallas	November, December, 1906	ULS
The New South	January, 1895	Galveston	January, 1895	Texas Collection, University of Texas
The Texas Magazine	May, 1896	Austin	April, 1898	ULS
Southern Home Magazine	May, 1897	Sherman	March, 1898	Texas Collection, University of Texas
The Southern Home Journal	May, 1898	Dallas	May, 1898	Texas Collection, University of Texas
The Bohemian	November, 1899	Fort Worth	Fall, 1907	Texas Collection, University of Texas; Baylor University; Library of Congress
Corona	August, 1901	Dallas	August, 1901	Public Library, Houston, Texas
Major's Magazine	April, 1902	Dallas	April, 1902	State Library, Nashville, Tennessee
Dixieland	February, 1904	Dallas	December, 1906	ULS
Harp of the West	March, 1904	Waco	March, 1904	Texas Collection, University of Texas
The American Home Journal	December, 1904	Dallas	June, 1915	ULS
The Southerner	March, 1905	Strawn	June, 1905	Texas Collection, University of Texas
The South	June, 1905	Dallas	October, 1908	Texas Collection, University of Texas
Holland's	August, 1905	Dallas	December, 1953	ULS
The American Woman's Home Journal	January, 1906	Dallas	January, 1906	Texas Collection, University of Texas
Our Mascot	April, 1906	San Antonio	August, 1906	Texas Collection, University of Texas
The Passing Show	November, 1906	San Antonio	January, 1912	ULS
The Green Book	May, 1908	Galveston	August, 1908	Texas Collection, University of Texas
Hunter's Frontier Magazine	November, 1910	Carlsbad	December, 1916	ULS
The Stylus	January, 1912	Houston	December, 1912	Texas Collection, University of Texas
International Magazine	April, 1912	San Antonio	May, 1912	ULS
The Texas Review— Southwest Review	June, 1915	Austin	Current	ULS
Grinstead's Graphic	January, 1921	Kerrville	December, 1925	ULS
Frontier Times	October, 1923	Bandera	Current	ULS
The Woman's Viewpoint	March, 1924	Houston	September, 1926	ULS
The Buccaneer	September, 1924	Dallas	July-December, 1926	ULS
The Texas Argus	March, 1928	San Antonio	April, 1928	Texas Collection, University of Texas
The Aclavache	March, 1929	Austin	March, 1929	Texas Collection, University of Texas

Index

Hartman, Miss Sara, 26, 27, 29
Harvey Carroll's Paper, 73
Hayne, Paul Hamilton, 5, 14
Heart o'the Hills Magazine, 88
Henry, O., 98
Hewlett, Maurice, 80
Higgins, Sheila Aden, ix
"High Private," H. P., 33, 34
Hobart, Sarah D., 12
Holland, Frank P., 59
Holland, Frank P., Jr., 59-61
Holland's, 59-61
Holly, Marietta, 12
Holt, Emily, 50
Houston, Percy, 78, 81
Houston, Texas, 2, 8, 26, 27, 29, 32, 55, 73, 75, 76, 94, 95, 98
Houston Post, The, 26
Houston Public Library, 2
Hubbell, Jay B., 82-85
Hughes, H. H., 60
Hughes, William Edgar, 36
Hunt, Leigh, 48
Hunter, J. Marvin, Jr., 92, 93
Hunter, J. Marvin, Sr., 71, 72, 90-93
Hunter, Jack M., 92
Hunter, John Warren, 71, 72
Hunter, Mrs. J. Marvin, Jr., 92
Hunter's Frontier Magazine, 72, 90
Hunter's Magazine of Frontier History, Border Tragedy, Pioneer Achievement, 71-72, 90
Hunter's Museum, 72, 92
Huntsville, Texas, 2
Hymers, Maude F., 45

Immigration Journal, 33
International Magazine, 67, 76-77
International Publishing Co., 77
Ivy, H. A., 17

Jayne, Juliet, 100
Jeffries, Charlie, 99, 100
Johnson, Adam R., 54
Johnson, Alvin S., 81
Johnson, Fred E., 51, 52
Johnston, Mary, 32
Jones, Easley S., 82
Jones, Howard Mumford, 82
Jones, Jerome K., 57
Jones, Johnnie A., 68
Jordan, John Clark, 82

Keasbey, Lindley Miller, 80
Keiper, I. A. F., 57, 58
Keith, Frances A., 100
Kendall, Herbert S., 50
Kent, Mrs. E. C., 19, 20
Kerrville, Texas, 4, 86, 88, 89
King, Karl, 76
Kit's London Letter, 27
Knapp Bros., 34
Knapp, R. F., 60
Kyger, John C. F., 24

LaCrosse, Wisconsin, 11
Ladies Messenger, The, 26, 29
Lane, W. Frances, 40
Lane Printing Company, 40
Lanier, Sidney, 22
Law, Margaret, 80, 81
Law, Robert Adger, 78, 81, 82, 85
Lawrence, Stewart, 38
Ledger, The, 30
Lee, Alice Louise, 63
Lee, James Ward, ix
Lee, Olive B., 30, 32
Lee's Magazine, 31-32
Lee's Texas Magazine, 30, 32
Leisy, Ernest E., 84
Levy, John V., 69, 70
Levy, M. M., 69
Lewis, J. M., 60
Library of Congress, 8, 11, 36, 67, 69
Library of Southern Literature, 55
"Life of Antonio Lopez de Santa Anna," 35, 36, 37
Linn, Mrs. Mac, 54
Literary Guardian, 9
Lloyd, Everett, 73
London, Jack, 67
Lone Star Magazine, The, 18
Louisiana, 27
Louisiana State University, 84
Louisville Courier-Journal, 30

McCleary, Robert E., 35-37
McClure, Mary, 28
McClure, 31
McComb and Bagby, Messrs., 9
McComb, W. P., 9, 10
Macdonald, Henry J., 7
Macfarland, Miss Alice, 73
McGinnis, John H., 82-84
McGraw, Theodosia, 73